Court of Protection Practice 2015

Court of Protection Rules 2007

incorporating the

Court of Protection (Amendment) Rules 2015

JORDAN PUBLISHING

Published by
Jordan Publishing Limited
21 St Thomas Street
Bristol BS1 6JS

British Library Cataloguing-in-Publication Data
A catalogue record for this book is available from the British Library.

ISSN 2040-2627

ISBN 978 1 78473 060 4

This volume is typeset by Letterpart Ltd, Caterham on the Hill, Surrey CR3 5XL

Printed in Great Britain by Hobbs the Printers Limited, Totton, Hampshire SO40 3WX

Court of Protection Rules 2007, SI 2007/1744

ARRANGEMENT OF RULES

PART 1
PRELIMINARY

Rule		Page
1	Title and commencement	10
2	Revocations	10
	PART 2 THE OVERRIDING OBJECTIVE	
3	The overriding objective	10
3A	Participation of P	11
4	*The duty of the parties*	11
4	The duty of the parties	12
5	Court's duty to manage cases	12
	PART 3 INTERPRETATION AND GENERAL PROVISIONS	
6	Interpretation	13
7	Court officers	15
7A		15
8	Computation of time	15
9	*Application of the Civil Procedure Rules*	15
9	Application of Civil Procedure Rules and Family Procedure Rules	16
9A	Pilot schemes	16
	PART 4 COURT DOCUMENTS	
10	Documents used in court proceedings	16
11	Documents required to be verified by a statement of truth	17
11A	Position statement not required to be verified by statement of truth	18
12	Failure to verify a document	18
13	Failure to verify a witness statement	18
14	False statements	18
15	Personal details	18
16	Supply of documents to a party from court records	19
17	Supply of documents to a non-party from court records	19
18	Subsequent use of court documents	19
19	Editing information in court documents	19
20	Public Guardian to be supplied with court documents relevant to supervision of deputies	19
21	Provision of court order to Public Guardian	20
22	Amendment of application	20
23	Clerical mistakes or slips	21
24	Endorsement of amendment	21
	PART 5 GENERAL CASE MANAGEMENT POWERS	
25	The court's general powers of case management	21
26	Court's power to dispense with requirement of any rule	22
27	Exercise of powers on the court's own initiative	22

28 General power of the court to rectify matters where there has been an error of procedure 22

PART 6
SERVICE OF DOCUMENTS

Service generally

29 Scope 22
30 Who is to serve 23
31 Methods of service 23
32 Service of documents on children and protected parties 24
33 Service of documents on P if he becomes a party 25
34 Substituted service 25
35 Deemed service 25
36 Certificate of service 26
37 Certificate of non-service 26
38 Power of court to dispense with service 26

Service out of the jurisdiction

39 Application of Family Procedure (Adoption) Rules 2005 27
39 Scope and interpretation 27
39A Service of application form and other documents out of the jurisdiction 28
39B Period for acknowledging service or responding to application where application is served out of the jurisdiction 28
39C Method of service – general provisions 28
39D Service in accordance with the Service Regulation 29
39E Service through foreign governments, judicial authorities and British Consular authorities 29
39F Procedure where service is to be through foreign governments, judicial authorities and British Consular authorities 30
39G Translation of application form or other document 31
39H Undertaking to be responsible for expenses of the Foreign and Commonwealth Office 31

PART 7
NOTIFYING P

General requirement to notify P

40 General 32
41 Who is to notify P 32
41A Notifying P of appointment of a litigation friend, etc 32

Circumstances in which P must be notified

42 Application forms 33
43 Appeals 33
44 Final orders 34
45 Other matters 34

Manner of notification, and accompanying documents

46 Manner of notification 34
47 Acknowledgment of notification 35
48 Certificate of notification 35
48 Certificate of notification 35
49 Dispensing with requirement to notify, etc 35

PART 8
PERMISSION

50 General 35

51 Where the court's permission is not required 36
51 Where the court's permission is not required 36
52 Exceptions to rule 51(2)(a) 36
53 Permission – supplementary 37
54 Application for permission 37
54 Application for permission 38
55 What the court will do when an application for permission to start proceedings is filed 38
56 Persons to be notified of the hearing of an application for permission 38
57 Acknowledgment of notification of permission application 38
58 Failure to file acknowledgment of notification 39
59 Service of an order giving or refusing permission 39
60 Appeal against a permission decision following a hearing 39

PART 9
HOW TO START PROCEEDINGS

Initial steps

61 General 40
62 When proceedings are started 40
63 Contents of the application form 40
64 Documents to be filed with the application form 40
65 What the court will do when an application form is filed 41
65 What the court will do when an application form is filed 41

Steps following issue of application form

66 Applicant to serve the application form on named respondents 41
67 Applications relating to lasting powers of attorney 41
68 Applications relating to enduring powers of attorney 42
69 Applicant to notify P of an application 43
70 Applicant to notify other persons of an application 43
71 Requirements for certain applications 43

Responding to an application

72 Responding to an application 43

The parties to the proceedings

73 Parties to the proceedings 44
74 Persons to be bound as if parties 45
75 Application to be joined as a party 45
76 Applications for removal as a party to proceedings 45

PART 10
APPLICATIONS WITHIN PROCEEDINGS

77 Types of applications for which the Part 10 procedure may be used 46
78 Application notice to be filed 46
79 What an application notice must include 47
80 Service of an application notice 47
81 Applications without notice 47
81A Security for costs 48
81B Conditions to be satisfied 48
81C Security for costs other than from the applicant 49
81D Security for costs of an appeal 49

Interim Remedies

82 Orders for interim remedies 49

PART 10A
DEPRIVATION OF LIBERTY

82A 50

PART 11
HUMAN RIGHTS

83 General 50

PART 12
DEALING WITH APPLICATIONS

84 Dealing with the application 50
85 Directions 51

Allocation of proceedings

86 Court's jurisdiction in certain kinds of case to be exercised by certain judges 52
86 Court's jurisdiction in certain kinds of case to be exercised by certain judges 52

Disputing the jurisdiction of the court

87 Procedure for disputing the court's jurisdiction 53
87A Permission required to withdraw proceedings 53

Participation in hearings

88 Participation in hearings 53

Reconsideration of court orders

89 Orders made without a hearing or without notice to any person 54

PART 13
HEARINGS

Private hearings

90 General rule – hearing to be in private 55
91 Court's general power to authorise publication of information about proceedings 55

Power to order a public hearing

92 Court's power to order that a hearing be held in public 56

Supplementary

93 Supplementary provisions relating to public or private hearings 56

PART 14
ADMISSIONS, EVIDENCE AND DEPOSITIONS

Admissions

94 Making an admission 57

Evidence

95 Power of court to control evidence 57
96 Evidence of witnesses – general rule 57
97 Written evidence – general rule 58
98 Evidence by video link or other means 58
99 Service of witness statements for use at final hearing 58
100 Form of witness statement 58
101 Witness summaries 58
102 Affidavit evidence 59

103 Form of affidavit 59
104 Affidavit made outside the jurisdiction 59
105 Notarial acts and instruments 59
106 Summoning of witnesses 59
107 Power of court to direct a party to provide information 60

Depositions

108 Evidence by deposition 60
109 Conduct of examination 61
110 Fees and expenses of examiners of the court 61
111 Examiners of the court 61
112 Enforcing attendance of a witness 62
113 Use of deposition at a hearing 62

Taking evidence outside the jurisdiction

114 Interpretation 62
115 Where a person to be examined is in another Regulation State 62
116 Where a person to be examined is out of the jurisdiction – letter of request 63

Section 49 reports

117 Reports under section 49 of the Act 64
118 Written questions to person making a report under section 49 64

PART 15
EXPERTS

119 References to expert 65
120 Restriction on filing an expert's report 65
121 Duty to restrict expert evidence 65
122 Experts – overriding duty to the court 65
123 Court's power to restrict expert evidence 65
124 General requirement for expert evidence to be given in a written report 66
125 Written questions to experts 66
126 Contents of expert's report 67
127 Use by one party of expert's report disclosed by another 67
128 Discussions between experts 67
129 Expert's right to ask court for directions 67
130 Court's power to direct that evidence is to be given by a single joint expert 68
131 Instructions to a single joint expert 68

PART 16
DISCLOSURE

132 Meaning of disclosure 68
133 General or specific disclosure 68
134 Procedure for general or specific disclosure 69
135 Ongoing duty of disclosure 69
136 Right to inspect documents 69
137 Inspection and copying of documents 70
138 Claim to withhold inspection or disclosure of document 70
139 Consequence of failure to disclose documents or permit inspection 70

PART 17
LITIGATION FRIEND

140 Who may act as a litigation friend 71
141 Requirement for a litigation friend 71
142 Litigation friend without a court order 71

143 Litigation friend by court order 72
144 Court's power to prevent a person from acting as litigation friend or to order change 72
145 Appointment of litigation friend by court order – supplementary 72
146 Procedure where appointment of litigation friend comes to an end – for a child or protected party 73
147 Procedure where appointment of litigation friend comes to an end – for P 73
148 Procedure where P ceases to lack capacity 74
149 Practice direction in relation to litigation friends 74

PART 17
LITIGATION FRIENDS AND RULE 3A REPRESENTATIVES

Section 1
Litigation friends

140 Who may act as a litigation friend 74
141 Requirement for a litigation friend 75
142 Litigation friend without a court order 75
143 Litigation friend by court order 76
144 Court's power to prevent a person from acting as a litigation friend or to bring an end to an appointment of a person as a litigation friend or to appoint another one 76
145 Appointment of litigation friend by court order – supplementary 76
145A Procedure where appointment of a litigation friend comes to an end for a child 77
146 Practice direction in relation to litigation friends 77

Section 2
Rule 3A representatives

146A Interpretation 77
147 Who may act as a rule 3A representative for P 77
148 Rule 3A representative by court order 78
148A Application by rule 3A representative or by P for directions 78
148B Court's power to prevent a person from acting as a rule 3A representative or to bring an end to an appointment of a person as a rule 3A representative or appoint another one 78
148C Appointment of rule 3A representative by court order – supplementary 79
149 Practice direction in relation to rule 3A representatives 79

PART 18
CHANGE OF SOLICITOR

150 Change of solicitor 79
151 Legally aided persons 80
152 Order that a solicitor has ceased to act 80
153 Removal of solicitor who has ceased to act on application of another party 80
154 Practice direction relating to change of solicitor 81

PART 19
COSTS

155 Interpretation 81
156 Property and affairs – the general rule 83
157 Personal welfare – the general rule 83
158 Apportioning costs – the general rule 83
159 Departing from the general rule 83
160 Rules about costs in the Civil Procedure Rules to apply 83

160 Rules about costs in the Civil Procedure Rules to apply 84
161 Detailed assessment of costs 85
162 Employment of a solicitor by two or more persons 85
163 Costs of the Official Solicitor 85
164 Procedure for assessing costs 85
165 Costs following P's death 85
166 Costs orders in favour of or against non-parties 86
167 Remuneration of a deputy, donee or attorney 86
168 Practice Direction as to costs 86

PART 20
APPEALS

169 Scope of this Part 86
169 Scope of this Part 86
170 Interpretation 87
171 Dealing with appeals 87
171A Destination of appeals 87
171B Permission to appeal – appeals to the Court of Appeal 88
172 Permission to appeal 88
172 Permission to appeal – other cases 89
172A Appeal against an order for committal to prison 89
173 Matters to be taken into account when considering an application for permission 89
174 Parties to comply with the practice direction 90
174 Power to treat application for permission to appeal as application for reconsideration under rule 89 90
175 Appellant's notice 90
176 Respondent's notice 91
177 Variation of time 91
178 Power of appeal judge on appeal 92
179 Determination of appeals 92
180 Allocation 92

Appeals to the Court of Appeal

181 Appeals against decision of a puisne judge of the High Court, etc 93
182 Second appeals 93

PART 21
ENFORCEMENT

183 Enforcement methods – general 93
184 Application of the Civil Procedure Rules 1998 *and RSC Orders* 93

Orders for committal

185 Contempt of court – generally 94
186 Application for order of committal 94
187 Oral evidence 94
188 Hearing for committal order 94
189 Power to suspend execution of committal order 95
190 Warrant for arrest 95
191 Discharge of person committed 95
192 Penal notices 95
193 Saving for other powers 95
194 Power of court to commit on its own initiative 96

PART 22
TRANSITORY AND TRANSITIONAL PROVISIONS

195 Transitory provision: applications by former receivers 96

196 Transitory provision: dealing with applications under rule 195 96
197 Appeal against a decision of a nominated officer 97
198 Application of Rules to proceedings within paragraphs 3 and 12 of Schedule 5 to the Act 97
199 Practice direction 97

PART 23
MISCELLANEOUS

200 Order or directions requiring a person to give security for discharge of functions 97
201 Objections to registration of an enduring power of attorney: request for directions 98
202 Disposal of property where P ceases to lack capacity 99

PART 1
PRELIMINARY

1 Title and commencement

These Rules may be cited as the Court of Protection Rules 2007 and come into force on 1 October 2007.

2 Revocations

The following rules are revoked –

(a) the Court of Protection Rules 2001; and
(b) the Court of Protection (Enduring Powers of Attorney) Rules 2001.

PART 2
THE OVERRIDING OBJECTIVE

3 The overriding objective

(1) These Rules have the overriding objective of enabling the court to deal with a case justly, having regard to the principles contained in the Act.

(2) The court will seek to give effect to the overriding objective when it –

(a) exercises any power under these Rules; or
(b) interprets any rule or practice direction.

(3) Dealing with a case justly includes, so far as is practicable –

(a) ensuring that it is dealt with expeditiously and fairly;
(b) ensuring that P's interests and position are properly considered;
(c) dealing with the case in ways which are proportionate to the nature, importance and complexity of the issues;
(d) ensuring that the parties are on an equal footing;
(e) saving expense; and
(f) allotting to it an appropriate share of the court's resources, while taking account of the need to allot resources to other cases.

[3A Participation of P]

[(1) The court shall in each case, on its own initiative or on the application of any person, consider whether it should make one or more of the directions in paragraph (2), having regard to –

(a) the nature and extent of the information before the court;
(b) the issues raised in the case;
(c) whether a matter is contentious; and
(d) whether P has been notified in accordance with the provisions of Part 7 and what, if anything, P has said or done in response to such notification.

(2) The directions are that –

(a) P should be joined as a party;
(b) P's participation should be secured by the appointment of an accredited legal representative to represent P in the proceedings and to discharge such other functions as the court may direct;
(c) P's participation should be secured by the appointment of a representative whose function shall be to provide the court with information as to the matters set out in section 4(6) of the Act and to discharge such other functions as the court may direct;
(d) P should have the opportunity to address (directly or indirectly) the judge determining the application and, if so directed, the circumstances in which that should occur;
(e) P's interests and position can properly be secured without any direction under sub-paragraphs (a) to (d) being made or by the making of an alternative direction meeting the overriding objective.

(3) Any appointment or directions made pursuant to paragraph (2)(b) to (e) may be made for such period or periods as the court thinks fit.

(4) Unless P has capacity to conduct the proceedings, an order joining P as a party shall only take effect

(a) on the appointment of a litigation friend on P's behalf; or
(b) if the court so directs, on or after the appointment of an accredited legal representative.

(5) If the court has directed that P should be joined as a party but such joinder does not occur because no litigation friend or accredited legal representative is appointed, the court shall record in a judgment or order –

(a) the fact that no such appointment was made; and
(b) the reasons given for that appointment not being made.

(6) A practice direction may make additional or supplementary provision in respect of any of the matters set out in this rule.

(The appointment of litigation friends, accredited legal representatives and representatives under paragraph (2)(c) is dealt with under Part 17.)

("Accredited legal representative" is defined in rule 6.)]

Amendments—Provision inserted with effect from 1 July 2015 by virtue of SI 2015/548.

4 The duty of the parties

The parties are required to help the court to further the overriding objective.

[4 The duty of the parties]

[(1) The parties are required to help the court to further the overriding objective.

(2) Without prejudice to the generality of paragraph (1), each party is required to –

- (a) co-operate with the other parties and with the court in identifying and narrowing the issues that need to be determined by the court, and the timetable for that determination;
- (b) adhere to the timetable set by these Rules and by the court;
- (c) comply with all directions and orders of the court;
- (d) be full and frank in the disclosure of information and evidence to the court (including any disclosure ordered under Part 16);
- (e) co-operate with the other parties in all aspects of the conduct of the proceedings, including in the preparation of bundles.

(3) If the court determines that any party has failed without reasonable excuse to satisfy the requirements of this rule, it may under rule 159 depart from the general rules about costs in so far as they apply to that party.

(Rule 133(2) deals with the requirements of general disclosure.)]

Amendments—Provision substituted with effect from 1 July 2015 by virtue of SI 2015/548.

5 Court's duty to manage cases

(1) The court will further the overriding objective by actively managing cases.

(2) Active case management includes –

- (a) encouraging the parties to co-operate with each other in the conduct of the proceedings;
- (b) identifying at an early stage –
  - (i) the issues; and
  - (ii) who should be a party to the proceedings;
- (c) deciding promptly –
  - (i) which issues need a full investigation and hearing and which do not; and
  - (ii) the procedure to be followed in the case;
- (d) deciding the order in which issues are to be resolved;
- (e) encouraging the parties to use an alternative dispute resolution procedure if the court considers that appropriate;
- (f) fixing timetables or otherwise controlling the progress of the case;
- (g) considering whether the likely benefits of taking a particular step justify the cost of taking it;
- (h) dealing with as many aspects of the case as the court can on the same occasion;
- (i) dealing with the case without the parties needing to attend at court;
- (j) making use of technology; *and*
- (k) giving directions to ensure that the case proceeds quickly and efficiently.[;
- (l) considering whether any hearing should be held in public; and
- (m) considering whether any document relating to proceedings should be a public document and, if so, whether and to what extent it should be redacted.

(Rules 91 to 93 make provision about the court's powers to authorise publication of information about proceedings and to order that a hearing be held in public.)]

Amendments—Word in italics revoked and words in square brackets inserted with effect from 1 July 2015 by virtue of SI 2015/548.

PART 3
INTERPRETATION AND GENERAL PROVISIONS

6 Interpretation

In these Rules –

'the Act' means the Mental Capacity Act 2005;

['accredited legal representative' means a legal representative authorised pursuant to a scheme of accreditation approved by the President to represent persons meeting the definition of 'P' in this rule in proceedings before the court;]

'applicant' means a person who makes, or who seeks permission to make, an application to the court;

'application form' means the document that is to be used to begin proceedings in accordance with Part 9 of these Rules or any other provision of these Rules or the practice directions which requires the use of an application form;

'application notice' means the document that is to be used to make an application in accordance with Part 10 of these Rules or any other provision of these Rules or the practice directions which requires the use of an application notice;

'attorney' means the person appointed as such by an enduring power of attorney created, or purporting to have been created, in accordance with the regulations mentioned in paragraph 2 of Schedule 4 to the Act;

'business day' means a day other than –

(a) a Saturday, Sunday, Christmas Day or Good Friday; or

(b) a bank holiday in England and Wales, under the Banking and Financial Dealings Act 1971;

'child' means a person under 18;

'court' means the Court of Protection;

'deputy' means a deputy appointed under the Act;

'donee' means the donee of a lasting power of attorney;

'donor' means the donor of a lasting power of attorney, except where this expression is used in rule 68 or 201(5) (where it means the donor of an enduring power of attorney);

'enduring power of attorney' means an instrument created in accordance with such of the regulations mentioned in paragraph 2 of Schedule 4 to the Act as applied when it was executed;

'filing' in relation to a document means delivering it, by post or otherwise, to the court office;

['hearing' includes a hearing conducted by telephone, video link, or any other method permitted or directed by the court;'judge' means a judge nominated to be a judge of the court under the Act;]

'lasting power of attorney' has the meaning given in section 9 of the Act;

'legal representative' means a –

(a) barrister,

(b) solicitor,

(c) solicitor's employee,

(d) manager of a body recognised under section 9 of the Administration of Justice Act 1985, or

(e) person who, for the purposes of the Legal Services Act 2007, is an authorised person in relation to an activity which constitutes the conduct of litigation (within the meaning of that Act),

who has been instructed to act for a party in relation to any application;

'legally aided person' means a person to whom civil legal services (within the meaning of the Legal Aid, Sentencing and Punishment of Offenders Act 2012) have been made available under arrangements made for the purposes of Part 1 of that Act);

'order' includes a declaration made by the court;

'P' means

(a) any person (other than a protected party) who lacks or, so far as consistent with the context, is alleged to lack capacity to make a decision or decisions in relation to any matter that is the subject of an application to the court; and

(b) a relevant person as defined by paragraph 7 of Schedule A1 to the Act,

and references to a person who lacks capacity are to be construed in accordance with the Act;

'party' is to be construed in accordance with rule 73;

'permission form' means the form that is to be used to make an application for permission to begin proceedings in accordance with Part 8 of these Rules;

'personal welfare' is to be construed in accordance with section 17 of the Act;

'President' and 'Vice-President' refer to those judges appointed as such under section 46(3)(a) and (b) of the Act;

'property and affairs' is to be construed in accordance with section 18 of the Act;

'protected party' means a party or an intended party (other than P or a child) who lacks capacity to conduct the proceedings;

['representative' means a person appointed under rule 3A(2)(c), except where the context otherwise requires;]

'respondent' means a person who is named as a respondent in the application form or notice, as the case may be;

'Senior Judge' means the judge who has been nominated to be Senior Judge under section 46(4) of the Act, and references in these Rules to a circuit judge include the Senior Judge;

['Tier 1 Judge' means any judge nominated to act as a judge of the Court of Protection under section 46 of the Act who is neither a Tier 2 Judge nor a Tier 3 Judge;

'Tier 2 Judge' means –

(a) the Senior Judge; and

(b) such other judges nominated to act as a judge of the Court of Protection under section 46 of the Act as may be set out in the relevant practice direction;

'Tier 3 Judge' means –

(a) the President;

(b) the Vice-President; and

(c) such other judges nominated to act as a judge of the Court of Protection under section 46 of the Act as may be set out in the relevant practice direction;]

'Visitor' means a person appointed as such by the Lord Chancellor under section 61 of the Act.

Amendment—Definitions of 'Tier 1 Judge', 'Tier 2 Judge' and 'Tier 3 Judge' inserted with effect from 6 April 2015 by virtue of SI 2015/548 (subject to transitional provisions). Definitions of 'accredited legal representative', 'hearing' and 'representative' inserted and definition of 'permission form' revoked (subject to transitional provisions) with effect from 1 July 2015 by virtue of SI 2015/548.

7 Court officers

(1) Where these Rules permit or require the court to perform an act of a purely formal or administrative character, that act may be performed by a court officer.

(2) A requirement that a court officer carry out any act at the request of any person is subject to the payment of any fee required by a fees order for the carrying out of that act.

7A (1) The Senior Judge or the President may authorise a court officer to exercise the jurisdiction of the court in such circumstances as set out in the relevant practice direction.

(2) A court officer who has been authorised under paragraph (1) –

- (a) must refer to a judge any application, proceedings or any question arising in any application or proceedings which ought, in the officer's opinion, to be considered by a judge;
- (b) may not deal with any application or proceedings or any question arising in any application or proceedings by way of a hearing; and
- (c) may not deal with an application for the reconsideration of an order made by that court officer or another court officer.

8 Computation of time

(1) This rule shows how to calculate any period of time which is specified –

- (a) by these Rules;
- (b) by a practice direction; or
- (c) in an order or direction of the court.

(2) A period of time expressed as a number of days must be computed as clear days.

(3) In this rule 'clear days' means that in computing the number of days –

- (a) the day on which the period begins; and
- (b) if the end of the period is defined by reference to an event, the day on which that event occurs,

are not included.

(4) Where the specified period is 7 days or less, and would include a day which is not a business day, that day does not count.

(5) When the specified period for doing any act at the court office ends on a day on which the office is closed, that act will be done in time if done on the next day on which the court office is open.

9 Application of the Civil Procedure Rules

In any case not expressly provided for by these Rules or the practice directions made under them, the Civil Procedure Rules 1998 (including any practice directions made under them) may be applied with any necessary modifications, insofar as is necessary to further the overriding objective.

[9 Application of Civil Procedure Rules and Family Procedure Rules]

[(1) In any case not expressly provided for by these Rules or the practice directions made under them, the court may apply either the Civil Procedure Rules 1998 or the Family Procedure Rules 2010 (including in either case the practice directions made under them) with any necessary modifications, in so far as is necessary to further the overriding objective.

(2) A reference in these Rules to the Civil Procedure Rules 1998 or to the Family Procedure Rules 2010 is to the version of those rules in force at the date specified for the purpose of that reference in the relevant practice direction.]

Amendments—Provision substituted with effect from 1 July 2015 by virtue of SI 2015/548.

[9A Pilot schemes]

[(1) Practice directions may make provision for the operation of pilot schemes for assessing the use of new practices and procedures in connection with proceedings –

- (a) for specified periods; and
- (b) in relation to proceedings –
  - (i) in specified parts of the country; or
  - (ii) relating to specified types of application.

(2) Practice directions may modify or disapply any provision of these Rules during the operation of such pilot schemes.]

Amendments—Provision inserted with effect from 1 July 2015 by virtue of SI 2015/548.

PART 4
COURT DOCUMENTS

10 Documents used in court proceedings

(1) The court will seal or otherwise authenticate with the stamp of the court the following documents on issue –

- *(a) a permission form;*
- (b) an application form;
- (c) an application notice;
- (d) an order; and
- (e) any other document which a rule or practice direction requires to be sealed or stamped.

(2) Where these Rules or any practice direction require a document to be signed, that requirement is satisfied if the signature is printed by computer or other mechanical means.

(3) A practice direction may make provision for documents to be filed or sent to the court by –

- (a) facsimile; or
- (b) other means.

Amendments—Words in italics revoked with effect from 1 July 2015 by virtue of SI 2015/548 (subject to transitional provisions).

11 Documents required to be verified by a statement of truth

(1) The following documents must be verified by a statement of truth –

(a) *a permission form, an application form or an application notice*[an application form, an application notice, an appellant's notice or a respondent's notice], where the applicant seeks to rely upon matters set out in the document as evidence;

(b) a witness statement;

(c) a certificate of –

(i) service or non-service; or

(ii) notification or non-notification;

(d) a deputy's declaration; and

(e) any other document required by a rule or practice direction to be so verified.

(2) Subject to paragraph (3), a statement of truth is a statement that –

(a) the party putting forward the document;

(b) in the case of a witness statement, the maker of the witness statement; or

(c) in the case of a certificate referred to in paragraph (1)(c), the person who signs the certificate,

believes that the facts stated in the document being verified are true.

(3) If a party is conducting proceedings with a litigation friend, the statement of truth in –

(a) a permission form;

(b) an application form; or

(c) an application notice*,*[;

(d) an appellant's notice or a respondent's notice]

is a statement that the litigation friend believes the facts stated in the document being verified are true.

(4) The statement of truth must be signed –

(a) in the case of *a permission form, an application form or an application notice*[an application form, an application notice, an appellant's notice or a respondent's notice] –

(i) by the party or litigation friend; or

(ii) by the legal representative on behalf of the party or litigation friend; and

(b) in the case of a witness statement, by the maker of the statement.

(5) A statement of truth which is not contained in the document which it verifies must clearly identify that document.

(6) A statement of truth in *a permission form, an application form or an application notice*[an application form, an application notice, an appellant's notice or a respondent's notice] may be made by –

(a) a person who is not a party; or

(b) two or more parties jointly,

where this is permitted by a relevant practice direction.

Amendments—Words in italics revoked and words in square brackets inserted with effect from 1 July 2015 by virtue of SI 2015/548 (subject to transitional provisions).

[11A Position statement not required to be verified by statement of truth]

[Nothing in these Rules requires a position statement to be verified by a statement of truth.]

Amendments—Provision inserted with effect from 1 July 2015 by virtue of SI 2015/548.

12 Failure to verify a document

If *a permission form, application form or application notice*[an application form, an application notice, an appellant's notice or a respondent's notice] is not verified by a statement of truth, the applicant [(or respondent as the case may be)] may not rely upon the document as evidence of any of the matters set out in it unless the court permits.

Amendments—Words in italics revoked and words in square brackets inserted with effect from 1 July 2015 by virtue of SI 2015/548 (subject to transitional provisions).

13 Failure to verify a witness statement

If a witness statement is not verified by a statement of truth, it shall not be admissible in evidence unless the court permits.

14 False statements

(1) Proceedings for contempt of court may be brought against a person if he makes, or causes to be made, a false statement in a document verified by a statement of truth without an honest belief in its truth.

(2) Proceedings under this rule may be brought only –

(a) by the Attorney General; or
(b) with the permission of the court.

15 Personal details

(1) Where a party does not wish to reveal –

(a) his home address or telephone number;
(b) P's home address or telephone number;
(c) the name of the person with whom P is living (if that person is not the applicant); or
(d) the address or telephone number of his place of business, or the place of business of any of the persons mentioned in sub-paragraphs (b) or (c),

he must provide those particulars to the court.

(2) Where paragraph (1) applies, the particulars given will not be revealed to any person unless the court so directs.

(3) Where a party changes his home address during the course of the proceedings, he must give notice of the change to the court.

(4) Where a party does not reveal his home address, he must nonetheless provide an address for service which must be within the jurisdiction of the court.

16 Supply of documents to a party from court records

Unless the court orders otherwise, a party to proceedings may inspect or obtain from the records of the court a copy of –

(a) any document filed by a party to the proceedings; or
(b) any communication in the proceedings between the court and –
  (i) a party to the proceedings; or
  (ii) another person.

17 Supply of documents to a non-party from court records

(1) Subject to rules 20 and 92(2), a person who is not a party to proceedings may inspect or obtain from the court records a copy of any judgment or order given or made in public.

(2) The court may, on an application made to it, authorise a person who is not a party to proceedings to –

(a) inspect any other documents in the court records; or
(b) obtain a copy of any such documents, or extracts from such documents.

(3) A person making an application for an authorisation under paragraph (2) must do so in accordance with Part 10.

(4) Before giving an authorisation under paragraph (2), the court will consider whether any document is to be provided on an edited basis.

18 Subsequent use of court documents

(1) Where a document has been filed or disclosed, a party to whom it was provided may use the document only for the purpose of the proceedings in which it was filed or disclosed, except where –

(a) the document has been read to or by the court or referred to at a public hearing; or
(b) the court otherwise permits.

(2) Paragraph (1)(a) is subject to any order of the court made under rule 92(2).

19 Editing information in court documents

(1) A party may apply to the court for an order that a specified part of a document is to be edited prior to the document's service or disclosure.

(2) An order under paragraph (1) may be made at any time.

(3) Where the court makes an order under this rule any subsequent use of that document in the proceedings shall be of the document as edited, unless the court directs otherwise.

(4) An application under this rule must be made in accordance with Part 10.

20 Public Guardian to be supplied with court documents relevant to supervision of deputies

(1) This rule applies in any case where the court makes an order –

(a) appointing a person to act as a deputy; or
(b) varying an order under which a deputy has been appointed.

(2) Subject to paragraphs (3) and (6), the Public Guardian is entitled to be supplied with a copy of qualifying documents if he reasonably considers that it is necessary for him to have regard to them in connection with the discharge of his functions under section 58 of the Act in relation to the supervision of deputies.

(3) The court may direct that the right to be supplied with documents under paragraph (2) does not apply in relation to such one or more documents, or descriptions of documents, as the court may specify.

(4) A direction under paragraph (3) or (6) may be given –

(a) either on the court's own initiative or on an application made to it; and
(b) either –
  (i) at the same time as the court makes the order which appoints the deputy, or which varies it; or
  (ii) subsequently.

(5) 'Qualifying documents' means documents which –

(a) are filed in court in connection with the proceedings in which the court makes the order referred to in paragraph (1); and
(b) are relevant to –
  (i) the decision to appoint the deputy;
  (ii) any powers conferred on him;
  (iii) any duties imposed on him; or
  (iv) any other terms applying to those powers and duties which are contained in the order.

(6) The court may direct that any document is to be provided to the Public Guardian on an edited basis.

21 Provision of court order to Public Guardian

Any order of the court requiring the Public Guardian to do something, or not to do something, will be served by the court on the Public Guardian as soon as practicable and in any event not later than 7 days after the order was made.

22 Amendment of application

(1) The court may allow or direct an applicant, at any stage of the proceedings, to amend his application form or notice.

(2) The amendment may be effected by making in writing the necessary alterations to the application form or notice, but if the amendments are so numerous or of such a nature or length that written alteration would make it difficult or inconvenient to read, a fresh document amended as allowed or directed may be issued.

23 Clerical mistakes or slips

The court may at any time correct any clerical mistakes in an order or direction or any error arising in an order or direction from any accidental slip or omission.

24 Endorsement of amendment

Where an application form or notice, order or direction has been amended under this Part, a note shall be placed on it showing the date on which it was amended and the alteration shall be sealed.

PART 5
GENERAL CASE MANAGEMENT POWERS

25 The court's general powers of case management

(1) The list of powers in this rule is in addition to any powers given to the court by any other rule or practice direction or by any other enactment or any powers it may otherwise have.

(2) The court may –

- (a) extend or shorten the time for compliance with any rule, practice direction, or court order or direction (even if an application for extension is made after the time for compliance has expired);
- (b) adjourn or bring forward a hearing;
- (c) require P, a party, a party's legal representative or litigation friend, to attend court;
- (d) hold a hearing and receive evidence by telephone or any other method of direct oral communication;
- (e) stay the whole or part of any proceedings or judgment either generally or until a specified date or event;
- (f) consolidate proceedings;
- (g) hear two or more applications on the same occasion;
- (h) direct a separate hearing of any issue;
- (i) decide the order in which issues are to be heard;
- (j) exclude an issue from consideration;
- (k) dismiss or give judgment on an application after a decision is made on a preliminary basis;
- (l) direct any party to file and serve an estimate of costs; and
- (m) take any step or give any direction for the purpose of managing the case and furthering the overriding objective.

(3) A judge to whom a matter is allocated may, if he considers that the matter is one which ought properly to be dealt with by another judge, transfer the matter to such a judge.

(4) Where the court gives directions it may take into account whether or not a party has complied with any rule or practice direction.

(5) The court may make any order it considers appropriate even if a party has not sought that order.

(6) A power of the court under these Rules to make an order includes a power to vary or revoke the order;

(7) Rules 25.12 to 25.15 of the Civil Procedure Rules 1998 (which make provision about security for costs) apply in proceedings to which these Rules apply as if the references in those Rules to 'defendant' and 'claimant' were to 'respondent' and 'applicant' respectively.

Amendments—Words in italics revoked with effect from 1 July 2015 by virtue of SI 2015/548.

26 Court's power to dispense with requirement of any rule

In addition to its general powers and the powers listed in rule 25, the court may dispense with the requirement of any rule.

27 Exercise of powers on the court's own initiative

(1) Except where these Rules or some other enactment make different provision, the court may exercise its powers on its own initiative.

(2) The court may make an order on its own initiative without hearing the parties or giving them the opportunity to make representations.

(3) Where the court proposes to make an order on its own initiative it may give the parties and any person it thinks fit an opportunity to make representations and, where it does so, it will specify the time by which, and the manner in which, the representations must be made.

(4) Where the court proposes –

(a) to make an order on its own initiative; and
(b) to hold a hearing to decide whether to make the order,

it will give the parties and may give any other person it thinks likely to be affected by the order at least 3 days' notice of the hearing.

28 General power of the court to rectify matters where there has been an error of procedure

Where there has been an error of procedure, such as a failure to comply with a rule or practice direction –

(a) the error does not invalidate any step taken in the proceedings unless the court so orders; and
(b) the court may waive the error or require it to be remedied or may make such other order as appears to the court to be just.

PART 6
SERVICE OF DOCUMENTS

Service generally

29 Scope

(1) Subject to paragraph (2), the rules in this Part apply to –

(a) the service of documents; and
(b) to the requirement under rule 70 for a person to be notified of the issue of an application form,

and references to 'serve', 'service', 'notice' and 'notify', and kindred expressions shall be construed accordingly.

(2) The rules in this Part do not apply where –

- (a) any other enactment, a rule in another Part or a practice direction makes different provision; or
- (b) the court directs otherwise.

30 Who is to serve

(1) The general rule is that the following documents will be served by the court –

- (a) an order or judgment of the court;
- (b) an acknowledgment of service or notification; and
- (c) except where the application is for an order for committal, a notice of hearing.

(2) Any other document is to be served by the party seeking to rely upon it, except where –

- (a) a rule or practice direction provides otherwise; or
- (b) the court directs otherwise.

(3) Where the court is to serve a document –

- (a) it is for the court to decide which of the methods of service specified in rule 31 is to be used; and
- (b) if the document is being served on behalf of a party, that party must provide sufficient copies.

31 Methods of service

(1) A document may be served by any of the methods specified in this rule.

(2) Where it is not known whether a solicitor is acting on behalf of a person, the document may be served by –

- (a) delivering it to the person personally;
- (b) delivering it at his home address or last known home address; or
- (c) sending it to that address, or last known address, by first class post (or by an alternative method of service which provides for delivery on the next working day).

(3) Where a solicitor –

- (a) is authorised to accept service on behalf of a person; and
- (b) has informed the person serving the document in writing that he is so authorised,

the document must be served on the solicitor, unless personal service is required by an enactment, rule, practice direction or court order.

(4) Where it appears to the court that there is a good reason to authorise service by a method other than those specified in paragraphs (2) or (3), the court may direct that service is effected by that method.

(5) A direction that service is effected by an alternative method must specify –

- (a) the method of service; and

(b) the date when the document will be deemed to be served.

(6) A practice direction may set out how documents are to be served by document exchange, electronic communication or other means.

32 Service of documents on children and protected parties

(1) The following table shows the person on whom a document must be served if it is a document which would otherwise be served on –

(a) a child; or
(b) a protected party.

Type of document	*Nature of party*	*Person to be served*
Application form	Child	A person who has parental responsibility for the child within the meaning of the Children Act 1989; or if there is no such person, a person with whom the child resides or in whose care the child is.
Application form	Protected party	The person who is authorised to conduct the proceedings in the protected party's name or on his behalf; or a person who is a duly appointed attorney, donee or deputy of the protected party; or if there is no such person, a person with whom the protected party lives or in whose care the latter is.
Application for an order appointing a litigation friend, where a child or protected party has no litigation friend	Child or protected party	See rule 145 (appointment of litigation friend by court order – supplementary).
Any other document	Child or protected party	The litigation friend or other duly authorised person who is conducting the proceedings on behalf of the child or protected party.

(2) The court may make an order for service on a child or a protected party by permitting the document to be served on some person other than the person specified in the table set out in paragraph (1) above (which may include service on the child or the protected party).

(3) An application for an order under paragraph (2) may be made without notice.

(4) The court may order that, although a document has been served on someone other than the person specified in the table, the document is to be treated as if it had been properly served.

(5) This rule does not apply in relation to the service of documents upon a child in any case where the court has made an order under rule 141(4) permitting the child to conduct proceedings without a litigation friend.

33 Service of documents on P if he becomes a party

(1) If P becomes a party to the proceedings, all documents to be served on him must be served on his litigation friend or *other person duly authorised to conduct proceedings*[as directed by the court] on P's behalf.

(2) The court may make an order for service on P by permitting the document to be served on some person other than the person specified in paragraph (1) above (which may include service on P).

(3) An application for an order under paragraph (2) may be made without notice.

(4) The court may order that, although a document has been served on someone other than a person specified in paragraph (1), the document is to be treated as if it had been properly served.

(5) This rule does not apply in relation to the service of documents upon P in any case where the court has made an order under rule *147(2) (procedure where appointment of a litigation friend comes to an end – for P)*[144(1)(b) (power of court to bring to an end the appointment of a litigation friend)].

> [(Rule 41A requires P to be notified where a direction has been made under rule 3A, and of the appointment of a litigation friend, accredited legal representative or representative.)]

Amendments—Words in italics revoked and words in square brackets inserted with effect from 1 July 2015 by virtue of SI 2015/548.

34 Substituted service

Where it appears to the court that it is impracticable for any reason to serve a document in accordance with any of the methods provided under rule 31, the court may make an order for substituted service of the document by taking such steps as the court may direct to bring it to the notice of the person to be served.

35 Deemed service

(1) A document which is served in accordance with these Rules or any relevant practice direction shall be deemed to be served on the day shown in the following table –

Method of service	*Deemed day of service*
First class post (or other service for next-day delivery)	The second day after it was posted.
Document exchange	The second day after it was left at the document exchange.
Delivering the document to a permitted address	The day after it was delivered to that address.

Method of service	*Deemed day of service*
Fax	If it is transmitted on a business day before 4 p.m., on that day; or in any other case, on the business day after the day on which it is transmitted.
Other electronic means	The second day after the day on which it is transmitted.

(2) If a document is served personally –

(a) after 5 p.m., on a business day; or
(b) at any time on a Saturday, Sunday or a Bank Holiday,

it will be treated as being served on the next business day.

36 Certificate of service

(1) Where a rule, practice direction or court order requires a certificate of service for the document, the certificate must state the details set out in the following table –

Method of service	*Details to be certified*
First class post (or any other service for next-day delivery)	Date of posting.
Personal service	Date of personal service
Document exchange	Date when the document was left at the document exchange.
Delivery of document to permitted address	Date when the document was delivered to that address.
Fax	Date of transmission.
Other electronic means	Date of transmission and the means used.
Alternative method permitted by the court	As required by the court.

(2) The certificate must be filed within 7 days after service of the document to which it relates.

37 Certificate of non-service

(1) Where an applicant or other person is unable to serve any document under these Rules or as directed by the court, he must file a certificate of non-service stating the reasons why service has not been effected.

(2) The certificate of non-service must be filed within 7 days of the latest date on which service should have been effected.

38 Power of court to dispense with service

(1) The court may dispense with any requirement to serve a document.

(2) An application for an order to dispense with service may be made without notice.

Service out of the jurisdiction

39 Application of Family Procedure (Adoption) Rules 2005

(1) The rules in Chapter 4 of Part 6 of the Family Procedure Rules 2010 ('the 2010 Rules') apply, with the modifications set out in this rule, to the service of documents out of the jurisdiction.

(2) References in the 2010 Rules to the Hague Convention shall be read in these Rules as references to the Convention on the International Protection of Adults signed at the Hague on 13th January 2000 (Cm. 5881).

(3) References in the 2010 Rules to the Senior Master of the Queen's Bench Division shall be read in these Rules as references to the Senior Judge.

[39 Scope and interpretation]

[(1) This rule and rules 39A to 39H make provision about –

(a) service of application forms and other documents out of the jurisdiction; and

(b) the procedure for service.

(2) In this rule and rules 39A to 39H –

'application form' includes an application notice;

'Commonwealth State' means a State listed in Schedule 3 to the British Nationality Act 1981;

'jurisdiction' means, unless the context otherwise requires, England and Wales and any part of the territorial waters of the United Kingdom adjoining England and Wales;

'Member State' means a Member State of the European Union;

'the Service Convention' means the Convention on the service abroad of judicial and extra-judicial documents in civil or commercial matters signed at the Hague on November 15, 1965;

'Service Convention country'means a country, not being a Member State, which is a party to the Service Convention; and

'the Service Regulation' means Regulation (EC) No 1393/2007 of the European Parliament and of the Council of 13 November 2007 on the service in the Member States of judicial and extra-judicial documents in civil and commercial matters (service of documents) and repealing Council Regulation (EC) No 1348/2000(2).

(3) In rules 39A to 39H, a reference to service by a party includes service by a person who is not a party where service by such a person is required under these Rules.]

Amendments—Provision substituted with effect from 1 July 2015 by virtue of SI 2015/548 (subject to transitional provisions).

[39A Service of application form and other documents out of the jurisdiction]

[(1) Subject to paragraph (2), any document to be served for the purposes of these Rules may be served out of the jurisdiction without the permission of the court.

(2) An application form may not be served out of the jurisdiction unless the court has power to determine the application to which it relates under the Act.]

Amendments—Provision inserted with effect from 1 July 2015 by virtue of SI 2015/548 (subject to transitional provisions).

[39B Period for acknowledging service or responding to application where application is served out of the jurisdiction]

[(1) This rule applies where, under these Rules, a party is required to file –

- (a) an acknowledgment of service; or
- (b) an answer to an application,

and sets out the time period for doing so where the application is served out of the jurisdiction.

(2) Where the applicant serves an application on a respondent in –

- (a) Scotland or Northern Ireland; or
- (b) a Member State or Service Convention country within Europe,

the period for filing an acknowledgment of service or an answer to an application is 21 days after service of the application.

(3) Where the applicant serves an application on a respondent in a Service Convention country outside Europe, the period for filing an acknowledgment of service or an answer to an application is 31 days after service of the application.

(4) Where the applicant serves an application on a respondent in a country not referred to in paragraphs (2) and (3), the period for filing an acknowledgment of service or an answer to an application is set out in Practice Direction 6B.]

Amendments—Provision inserted with effect from 1 July 2015 by virtue of SI 2015/548 (subject to transitional provisions).

[39C Method of service – general provisions]

[(1) This rule contains general provisions about the method of service of an application form or other document on a party out of the jurisdiction.

Where service is to be effected on a party in Scotland or Northern Ireland

(2) Where a party serves an application form or other document on a party in Scotland or Northern Ireland, it must be served by a method permitted by this Part.

Where service is to be effected out of the United Kingdom

(3) Where an application form or other document is to be served on a person out of the United Kingdom, it may be served by any method –

- (a) provided for by –
  - (i) rule 39D (service in accordance with the Service Regulation); or
  - (ii) rule 39E (service through foreign governments, judicial authorities and British Consular authorities); or

(b) permitted by the law of the country in which it is to be served.

(4) Nothing in paragraph (3) or in any court order authorises or requires any person to do anything which is contrary to the law of the country where the application form or other document is to be served.]

Amendments—Provision inserted with effect from 1 July 2015 by virtue of SI 2015/548 (subject to transitional provisions).

[39D Service in accordance with the Service Regulation]

[(1) This rule applies where an application form or other document is to be served on a person out of the United Kingdom in accordance with the Service Regulation.

(2) The person wishing to serve must file –

(a) the application form or other document;
(b) any translation; and
(c) any other documents required by the Service Regulation.

(3) When the person wishing to serve files the documents referred to in paragraph (2), the court officer must –

(a) seal, or otherwise authenticate with the stamp of the court, the copy of the application form; and
(b) forward the documents to the Senior Master of the Queen's Bench Division.

(4) In addition to the documents referred to in paragraph (2), the person wishing to serve may, if of the view that this would assist in ensuring effective service, file a photograph of the person to be served.

(The Service Regulation is annexed to Practice Direction 6B.)

(Rule 39E makes provision for service on a person in a Service Convention country.)]

Amendments—Provision inserted with effect from 1 July 2015 by virtue of SI 2015/548 (subject to transitional provisions).

[39E Service through foreign governments, judicial authorities and British Consular authorities]

[(1) Where an application form or other document is to be served on a person in a Service Convention country, it may be served –

(a) through the authority designated under the Service Convention in respect of that country; or
(b) if the law of that country permits, through –
   (i) the judicial authorities of that country; or
   (ii) a British Consular authority in that country.

(2) Where an application form or other document is to be served on a person in a country which is not a Service Convention country, it may be served, if the law of that country so permits, through –

(a) the government of that country, where that government is willing to serve it; or
(b) a British Consular authority in that country.

(3) Where an application form or other document is to be served in –

(a) any Commonwealth State which is not a Service Convention country;
(b) the Isle of Man or the Channel Islands; or
(c) any British Overseas Territory,

the methods of service permitted by paragraphs (1)(b) and (2) are not available and the person wishing to serve, or that person's agent, must effect service direct unless Practice Direction 6B provides otherwise.

(4) This rule does not apply where service is to be effected in accordance with the Service Regulation.

(Rule 39D makes provision for service on a party in a Member State in accordance with the Service Regulation.)

(A list of British Overseas Territories is reproduced in Practice Direction 6B.)]

Amendments—Provision inserted with effect from 1 July 2015 by virtue of SI 2015/548 (subject to transitional provisions).

[39F Procedure where service is to be through foreign governments, judicial authorities and British Consular authorities]

[(1) This rule applies where an application form or other document is to be served under rule 39E(1) or (2).

(2) Where this rule applies, the person wishing to serve must file –

(a) a request for service of the application form or other document, by specifying one or more of the methods in rule 39E(1) or (2);
(b) a copy of the application form or other document;
(c) any other documents or copies of documents required by Practice Direction 6B; and
(d) any translation required under rule 39G.

(3) When the person wishing to serve files the documents specified in paragraph (2), the court officer must –

(a) seal, or otherwise authenticate with the stamp of the court, the copy of the application form; and
(b) forward the documents to the Senior Master of the Queen's Bench Division.

(4) The Senior Master shall send documents forwarded under this rule –

(a) where the application form or other document is being served through the authority designated under the Service Convention, to that authority; or
(b) in any other case, to the Foreign and Commonwealth Office with a request that it arranges for the application form or other document to be served.

(5) An official certificate which –

(a) states that the method requested under paragraph (2)(a) has been performed and the date of such performance;
(b) states, where more than one method is requested under paragraph (2)(a), which method was used; and
(c) is made by –
    (i) a British Consular authority in the country where the method requested under paragraph (2)(a) was performed;
    (ii) the government or judicial authorities in that country; or

(iii) the authority designated in respect of that country under the Service Convention,

is evidence of the facts stated in the certificate.

(6) A document purporting to be an official certificate under paragraph (5) is to be treated as such a certificate unless it is proved not to be.]

Amendments—Provision inserted with effect from 1 July 2015 by virtue of SI 2015/548 (subject to transitional provisions).

[39G Translation of application form or other document]

[(1) Except where paragraphs (4) and (5) apply, every copy of the application form or other document filed under rule 39E (service through foreign governments, judicial authorities and British Consular authorities) must be accompanied by a translation of the application form or other document.

(2) The translation must be –

(a) in the official language of the country in which it is to be served; or
(b) if there is more than one official language of that country, in any official language which is appropriate to the place in the country where the application form or other document is to be served.

(3) Every translation filed under this rule must be accompanied by a statement by the person making it that it is a correct translation, and the statement must include that person's name, address and qualifications for making the translation.

(4) The applicant is not required to file a translation of the application form or other document filed under rule 39E where it is to be served in a country of which English is an official language.

(5) The applicant is not required to file a translation of the application form or other document filed under rule 39E where –

(a) the person on whom the document is to be served is able to read and understand English; and
(b) service of the document is to be effected directly on that person.

(This rule does not apply to service in accordance with the Service Regulation, which contains its own provisions about the translation of documents.)]

Amendments—Provision inserted with effect from 1 July 2015 by virtue of SI 2015/548 (subject to transitional provisions).

[39H Undertaking to be responsible for expenses of the Foreign and Commonwealth Office]

[Every request for service under rule 39F (procedure where service is to be through foreign governments, judicial authorities, etc) must contain an undertaking by the person making the request –

(a) to be responsible for all expenses incurred by the Foreign and Commonwealth Office or foreign judicial authority; and .
(b) to pay those expenses to the Foreign and Commonwealth Office or foreign judicial authority on being informed of the amount.]

Amendments—Provision inserted with effect from 1 July 2015 by virtue of SI 2015/548 (subject to transitional provisions).

PART 7
NOTIFYING P

General requirement to notify P

40 General

(1) Subject to paragraphs (2) and (3), the rules in this Part apply where P is to be given notice of any matter or document, or is to be provided with any document, either under the Rules or in accordance with an order or direction of the court.

(2) *If*[Except where rule 41A applies, if] P becomes a party, the rules in this Part do not apply and service is to be effected in accordance with Part 6 or as directed by the court.

(3) In any case the court may, either on its own initiative or on application, direct that P must not be notified of any matter or document, or provided with any document, whether in accordance with this Part or at all.

[(4) Subject to paragraph (5), where P is a child—

- (a) if the person to be notified under this rule is a person with parental responsibility for the child within the meaning of the Children Act 1989 or, if there is no such person, a person with whom the child resides or in whose care the child is;
- (b) all references to "P" in this Part, except that in paragraph (2), are to be read as referring to the person notified in accordance with sub-paragraph (a).

(5) Paragraph (4) does not apply, and there is no requirement to notify P, where the person referred to in paragraph (4)(a) has already been served or notified of the relevant matter in accordance with another rule or practice direction.]

Amendments—Word in italics revoked and words in square brackets inserted with effect from 1 July 2015 by virtue of SI 2015/548 (subject to transitional provisions).

41 Who is to notify P

(1) Where P is to be notified under this Part, notification must be effected by –

- (a) the applicant;
- (b) the appellant (where the matter relates to an appeal);
- (c) an agent duly appointed by the applicant or the appellant; or
- (d) such other person as the court may direct.

(2) The person within paragraph (1) is referred to in this Part as 'the person effecting notification'.

[41A Notifying P of appointment of a litigation friend, etc]

[P must be notified –

- (a) where a direction has been made under rule 3A; and
- (b) of the appointment of a litigation friend, accredited legal representative or representative on P's behalf.]

Amendments—Provision inserted with effect from 1 July 2015 by virtue of SI 2015/548 (subject to transitional provisions).

Circumstances in which P must be notified

42 Application forms

(1) P must be notified-

(a) that an application form has been issued by the court;
(b) that an application form has been withdrawn; and
(c) of the date on which a hearing is to be held in relation to the matter, where that hearing is for disposing of the application.

(2) Where P is to be notified that an application form has been issued, the person effecting notification must explain to P –

(a) who the applicant is;
(b) that the application raises the question of whether P lacks capacity in relation to a matter or matters, and what that means;
(c) what will happen if the court makes the order or direction that has been applied for; and
(d) where the application contains a proposal for the appointment of a person to make decisions on P's behalf in relation to the matter to which the application relates, details of who that person is.

(3) Where P is to be notified that an application form has been withdrawn, the person effecting notification must explain to P –

(a) that the application form has been withdrawn; and
(b) the consequences of that withdrawal.

(4) The person effecting notification must also inform P that he may seek advice and assistance in relation to any matter of which he is notified.

43 Appeals

(1) P must be notified –

(a) that an appellant's notice has been issued by the court;
(b) that an appellant's notice has been withdrawn; and
(c) of the date on which a hearing is to be held in relation to the matter, where that hearing is for disposing of the appellant's notice.

(2) Where P is to be notified that an appellant's notice has been issued, the person effecting notification must explain to P –

(a) who the appellant is;
(b) the issues raised by the appeal; and
(c) what will happen if the court makes the order or direction that has been applied for.

(3) Where P is to be notified that an appellant's notice has been withdrawn, the person effecting notification must explain to P –

(a) that the appellant's notice has been withdrawn; and
(b) the consequences of that withdrawal.

(4) The person effecting notification must also inform P that he may seek advice and assistance in relation to any matter of which he is notified.

44 Final orders

(1) P must be notified of *a final order of the court*[any decision of the court relating to P except for a case management decision].

(2) Where P is notified in accordance with this rule, the person effecting notification must explain to P the effect of the *order*[decision].

(3) The person effecting notification must also inform P that *he*[P] may seek advice and assistance in relation to any matter of which *he*[P] is notified.

[(4) The person effecting notification must also provide P with a copy of any order relating to a decision of which P must be notified in accordance with paragraph (1).]

Amendments—Words in italics revoked and words in square brackets inserted with effect from 1 July 2015 by virtue of SI 2015/548 (subject to transitional provisions).

45 Other matters

(1) This rule applies where the court directs that P is to be notified of any other matter.

(2) The person effecting notification must explain to P such matters as may be directed by the court.

(3) The person effecting notification must also inform P that he may seek advice and assistance in relation to any matter of which he is notified.

Manner of notification, and accompanying documents

46 Manner of notification

(1) Where P is to be notified under this Part, the person effecting notification must provide P with[, or arrange for P to be provided with,] the information specified in rules *42*[41A] to 45 in a way that is appropriate to P's circumstances (for example, using simple language, visual aids or any other appropriate means).

(2) The information referred to in paragraph (1) must be provided to P personally.

(3) P must be provided with the information mentioned in paragraph (1) as soon as practicable and in any event within *21*[14] days of the date on which –

- (a) the application form or appellant's notice was issued or withdrawn;
- (b) the *order*[decision] was made; *or*
- (c) the person effecting notification received the notice of hearing from the court and in any event no later than 14 days before the date specified in the notice of the hearing,[; and
- (d) the order referred to in rule 44(4) was served upon the person who is required to effect notification of P under that rule,]

as the case may be.

[(4) Where the provisions of rule 40(4) apply, paragraphs (1) and (2) of this rule do not apply and the person effecting notification may provide information and documents of which P must be notified to the person to be notified under rule 40(4), by any method by which service of documents would be permitted under rule 31.]

Amendments—Words in italics revoked and words in square brackets inserted with effect from 1 July 2015 by virtue of SI 2015/548 (subject to transitional provisions).

47 Acknowledgment of notification

When P is notified that an application form or an appellant's notice has been issued, he must also be provided with a form for acknowledging notification.

48 Certificate of notification

The person effecting notification must, within 7 days beginning with the date on which notification in accordance with this Part was given, file a certificate of notification which certifies –

(a) the date on which P was notified; and
(b) that he was notified in accordance with this Part.

[48 Certificate of notification]

[(1) The person effecting notification must, within 7 days beginning with the date on which notification in accordance with this Part was given, file a certificate of notification which certifies –

(a) the date on which, and how, P was notified; and
(b) that P was notified in accordance with this Part.

(2) Subject to paragraph (3), the person effecting notification in accordance with this Part must in the certificate required by paragraph (1) describe the steps taken to enable P to understand, and the extent to which P appears to have understood, the information.

(3) Where the provisions of rule 40(4) apply, paragraph (2) does not apply.]

Amendments—Provision substituted with effect from 1 July 2015 by virtue of SI 2015/548 (subject to transitional provisions).

49 Dispensing with requirement to notify, etc

(1) The applicant, the appellant or other person directed by the court to effect notification may apply to the court seeking an order –

(a) dispensing with the requirement to comply with the provisions in this Part; or
(b) requiring some other person to comply with the provisions in this Part.

(2) An application under this rule must be made in accordance with Part 10.

PART 8
PERMISSION

50 General

Subject to these Rules and to section 50(1) of, and paragraph 20 of Schedule 3 to, the Act, the applicant must apply for permission to start proceedings under the Act.

(Section 50(1) of the Act specifies persons who do not need to apply for permission. Paragraph 20 of Schedule 3 to the Act specifies an application for which permission is not needed.)

51 Where the court's permission is not required

The permission of the court is not required –

(1) where an application is made by –

- *(a) the Official Solicitor; or*
- *(b) the Public Guardian;*

(2) where the application concerns –

- *(a) P's property and affairs, unless the application is of a kind specified in rule 52;*
- *(b) a lasting power of attorney which is, or purports to be, created under the Act; or*
- *(c) an instrument which is, or purports to be, an enduring power of attorney;*

(2A) where an application is made under section 21A of the Act by the relevant person's representative;]

(3) where an application is made in accordance with Part 10; or

(4) where a person files an acknowledgment of service or notification in accordance with this Part or Part 9, for any order proposed that is different from that sought by the applicant.

[51 Where the court's permission is not required]

[The permission of the court is not required –

- (a) where an application is made by –
  - (i) the Official Solicitor; or
  - (ii) the Public Guardian;
- (b) where the application concerns –
  - (i) P's property and affairs;
  - (ii) a lasting power of attorney which is, or purports to be, created under the Act; or
  - (iii) an instrument which is, or purports to be, an enduring power of attorney;
- (c) where an application is made under section 21A of the Act;
- (d) where an application is made for an order under section 16(2)(a) of the Act, which is to be relied on to authorise the deprivation of P's liberty pursuant to section 4A(3) of the Act;
- (e) where an application is made in accordance with Part 10;
- (f) where a person files an acknowledgment of service or notification in accordance with this Part or Part 9, for any order proposed that is different from that sought by the applicant; or
- (g) in any other case specified for this purpose in a practice direction.]

Amendments—Provision substituted with effect from 1 July 2015 by virtue of SI 2015/548 (subject to transitional provisions).

52 Exceptions to rule 51(2)(a)

(1) For the purposes of rule 51(2)(a), the permission of the court is required to make any of the applications specified in this rule.

(2) An application for the exercise of the jurisdiction of the court under section 54(2) of the Trustee Act 1925, where the application is made by a person other than –

- *(a) a person who has made an application for the appointment of a deputy;*
- *(b) a continuing trustee; or*
- *(c) any other person who, according to the practice of the Chancery Division, would have been entitled to make the application if it had been made in the High Court.*

(3) An application under section 36(9) of the Trustee Act 1925 for leave to appoint a new trustee in place of P, where the application is made by a person other than –

- *(a) a co-trustee; or*
- *(b) another person with the power to appoint a new trustee.*

(4) An application seeking the exercise of the court's jurisdiction under section 18(1)(b) (where the application relates to making a gift of P's property), (h) or (i) of the Act, where the application is made by a person other than –

- *(a) a person who has made an application for the appointment of a deputy;*
- *(b) a person who, under any known will of P or under his intestacy, may become entitled to any property of P or any interest in it;*
- *(c) a person who is an attorney appointed under an enduring power of attorney which has been registered in accordance with the Act or the regulations referred to in Schedule 4 to the Act;*
- *(d) a person who is a donee of a lasting power of attorney which has been registered in accordance with the Act; or*
- *(e) a person for whom P might be expected to provide if he had capacity to do so.*

(5) An application under section 20 of the Trusts of Land and Appointment of Trustees Act 1996, where the application is made by a person other than a beneficiary under the trust or, if there is more than one, by both or all of them.

Amendments—Provision revoked with effect from 1 July 2015 by virtue of SI 2015/548 (subject to transitional provisions).

53 Permission – supplementary

(1) The provisions of rule 52(2) apply with such modifications as may be necessary to an application under section 18(1)(j) of the Act for an order for the exercise of any power vested in P of appointing trustees or retiring from a trust.

(2) Where part of the application concerns a matter which requires permission, and part of it does not, permission need only be sought for that part of it which requires permission.

Amendments—Words in italics revoked with effect from 1 July 2015 by virtue of SI 2015/548 (subject to transitional provisions).

54 Application for permission

The applicant must apply for permission by filing a permission form and must file with it –

- *(a) any information or documents specified in the relevant practice direction;*

(b) a draft of the application form which he seeks permission to have issued; and

(c) an assessment of capacity form, where this is required by the relevant practice direction.

[54 Application for permission]

[Where permission is required, the applicant must apply for permission when making an application.

(Rule 84(1A) explains how the court will deal with an application for permission.)]

Amendments—Provision substituted with effect from 1 July 2015 by virtue of SI 2015/548 (subject to transitional provisions).

55 What the court will do when an application for permission to start proceedings is filed

Within 14 days of a permission form being filed, the court will issue it and –

(a) grant the application in whole or in part, or subject to conditions, without a hearing and may give directions in connection with the issue of the application form;

(b) refuse the application without a hearing; or

(c) fix a date for the hearing of the application.

Amendments—Provision revoked with effect from 1 July 2015 by virtue of SI 2015/548 (subject to transitional provisions).

56 Persons to be notified of the hearing of an application for permission

(1) Where the court fixes a date for a hearing under rule 55(c), it will notify the applicant and such other persons as it thinks fit, and provide them with –

(a) subject to paragraph (2), the documents mentioned in rule 54; and

(b) a form for acknowledging notification.

(2) The court may direct that any document is to be provided on an edited basis.

Amendments—Provision revoked with effect from 1 July 2015 by virtue of SI 2015/548 (subject to transitional provisions).

57 Acknowledgment of notification of permission application

(1) Any person who is notified of an application for permission and who wishes to take part in the permission hearing must file an acknowledgment of notification in accordance with the following provisions of this rule.

(2) The acknowledgment of notification must be filed not more than 21 days after notice of the application was given.

(3) The court will serve the acknowledgment of notification on the applicant and on any other person who has filed such an acknowledgment.

(4) The acknowledgment of notification must –

(a) state whether the person acknowledging notification consents to the application for permission;
(b) state whether he opposes the application for permission, and if so, set out the grounds for doing so;
(c) state whether he proposes that permission should be granted to make an application for a different order, and if so, set out what that order is;
(d) provide an address for service, which must be within the jurisdiction of the court; and
(e) be signed by him or his legal representative.

(5) The acknowledgment of notification may include or be accompanied by an application for directions.

(6) Subject to rules 120 and 123 (restrictions on filing an expert's report and court's power to restrict expert evidence), where a person opposes the application for permission or proposes that permission is granted for a different order, the acknowledgment of notification must be accompanied by a witness statement containing any evidence upon which that person intends to rely.

Amendments—Provision revoked with effect from 1 July 2015 by virtue of SI 2015/548 (subject to transitional provisions).

58 Failure to file acknowledgment of notification

Where a person notified of the application for permission has not filed an acknowledgment of notification in accordance with rule 57, he may not take part in a hearing to decide whether permission should be given unless the court permits him to do so.

Amendments—Provision revoked with effect from 1 July 2015 by virtue of SI 2015/548 (subject to transitional provisions).

59 Service of an order giving or refusing permission

The court *will*[must] serve –

(a) the order granting or refusing permission;
(b) if refusing permission without a hearing, the reasons for its decision in summary form; and
(c) any directions,

on the applicant and on any other person *notified of the application who filed an acknowledgment of notification*[served with or notified of the application form].

Amendments—Words in italics revoked and words in square brackets inserted with effect from 1 July 2015 by virtue of SI 2015/548 (subject to transitional provisions).

60 Appeal against a permission decision following a hearing

Where the court grants or refuses permission following a hearing, any appeal against the permission decision shall be dealt with in accordance with Part 20 (appeals).

> [(Rule 89 deals with reconsideration of orders and decisions made without a hearing or without notice to any person who is affected by such order or decision.)]

Amendments—Words in square brackets inserted with effect from 1 July 2015 by virtue of SI 2015/548 (subject to transitional provisions).

PART 9
HOW TO START PROCEEDINGS

Initial steps

61 General

(1) Applications to the court to start proceedings shall be made in accordance with this Part and, as applicable, Part 8 and the relevant practice directions.

(2) The appropriate forms must be used in the cases to which they apply, with such variations as the case requires, but not so as to omit any information or guidance which any form gives to the intended recipient.

(3) If permission to make an application is required, the court shall not issue the application form until permission is granted.

Amendments—Words in italics revoked with effect from 1 July 2015 by virtue of SI 2015/548 (subject to transitional provisions).

62 When proceedings are started

(1) The general rule is that proceedings are started when the court issues an application form at the request of the applicant.

(2) An application form is issued on the date entered on the application form by the court.

63 Contents of the application form

The application form must –

(a) state the matter which the applicant wants the court to decide;
(b) state the order which the applicant is seeking;
(c) name –
  (i) the applicant;
  (ii) P;
  (iii) as a respondent, any person (other than P) whom the applicant reasonably believes to have an interest which means that he ought to be heard in relation to the application (as opposed to being notified of it in accordance with rule 70); and
  (iv) any person whom the applicant intends to notify in accordance with rule 70; and
(d) if the applicant is applying in a representative capacity, state what that capacity is.

64 Documents to be filed with the application form

When an applicant files his application form with the court, he must also file –

(a) in accordance with the relevant practice direction, any evidence upon which he intends to rely;

(b) *if permission was required to make the application, a copy of the court's order granting permission;*
(c) an assessment of capacity form, where this is required by the relevant practice direction;
(d) any other documents referred to in the application form; and
(e) such other information and material as may be set out in a practice direction.

Amendments—Words in italics revoked with effect from 1 July 2015 by virtue of SI 2015/548 (subject to transitional provisions).

65 What the court will do when an application form is filed

As soon as practicable after an application form is filed the court will issue the application form in any case where permission –

(a) is not required; or
(b) has been granted by the court; and

do anything else that may be set out in a practice direction.

[65 What the court will do when an application form is filed]

[As soon as practicable after an application form is filed the court must issue it and do anything else that may be set out in a practice direction.]

Amendments—Provision substituted with effect from 1 July 2015 by virtue of SI 2015/548 (subject to transitional provisions).

Steps following issue of application form

66 Applicant to serve the application form on named respondents

(1) As soon as practicable and in any event within *21*[14] days of the date on which the application form was issued, the applicant must serve a copy of the application form on any person who is named as a respondent in the application form, together with copies of any documents filed in accordance with rule 64 and a form for acknowledging service.

(2) The applicant must file a certificate of service within 7 days beginning with the date on which the documents were served.

Amendments—Word in italics revoked and word in square brackets inserted with effect from 1 July 2015 by virtue of SI 2015/548 (subject to transitional provisions).

67 Applications relating to lasting powers of attorney

(1) Where the application concerns the powers of the court under section 22 or 23 of the Act (powers of the court in relation to the validity and operation of lasting powers of attorney) the applicant must serve a copy of the application form, together with copies of any documents filed in accordance with rule 64 and a form for acknowledging service –

(a) unless the applicant is the donor or donee of the lasting power of attorney ('the power'), on the donor and every donee of the power;

(b) if he is the donor, on every donee of the power; and
(c) if he is a donee, on the donor and any other donee of the power,

but only if the above-mentioned persons have not been served or notified under any other rule.

(2) Where the application is solely in respect of an objection to the registration of a power, the requirements of rules 66 and 70 do not apply to an application made under this rule by –

(a) a donee of the power; or
(b) a person named in a statement made by the donor of the power in accordance with paragraph 2(1)(c)(i) of Schedule 1 to the Act.

(3) The applicant must comply with paragraph (1) as soon as practicable and in any event within *21*[14] days of date on which the application form was issued.

(4) The applicant must file a certificate of service within 7 days beginning with the date on which the documents were served.

(5) Where the applicant knows or has reasonable grounds to believe that the donor of the power lacks capacity to make a decision in relation to any matter that is the subject of the application, he must notify the donor in accordance with Part 7.

Amendments—Word in italics revoked and word in square brackets inserted with effect from 1 July 2015 by virtue of SI 2015/548 (subject to transitional provisions).

68 Applications relating to enduring powers of attorney

(1) Where the application concerns the powers of the court under paragraphs 2(9), 4(5)(a) and (b), 7(2), 10(c), 13, or 16(2), (3), (4) and (6) of Schedule 4 to the Act, the applicant must serve a copy of the application form, together with copies of any documents filed in accordance with rule 64 and a form for acknowledging service –

(a) unless the applicant is the donor or attorney under the enduring power of attorney ('the power'), on the donor and every attorney of the power;
(b) if he is the donor, on every attorney under the power; or
(c) if he is an attorney, on the donor and any other attorney under the power,

but only if the above-mentioned persons have not been served or notified under any other rule.

(2) Where the application is solely in respect of an objection to the registration of a power, the requirements of rules 66 and 70 do not apply to an application made under this rule by –

(a) an attorney under the power; or
(b) a person listed in paragraph 6(1) of Schedule 4 to the Act.

(3) The applicant must comply with paragraph (1) as soon as practicable and in any event within *21*[14] days of the date on which the application form was issued.

(4) The applicant must file a certificate of service within 7 days beginning with the date on which the documents were served.

(5) Where the applicant knows or has reasonable grounds to believe that the donor of the power lacks capacity to make a decision in relation to any matter that is the subject of the application, he must notify the donor in accordance with Part 7.

Amendments—Word in italics revoked and word in square brackets inserted with effect from 1 July 2015 by virtue of SI 2015/548 (subject to transitional provisions).

69 Applicant to notify P of an application

P must be notified in accordance with Part 7 that an application form has been issued, unless the requirement to do so has been dispensed with under rule 49.

70 Applicant to notify other persons of an application

(1) As soon as practicable and in any event within *21*[14] days of the date on which the application form was issued, the applicant must notify the persons specified in the relevant practice direction –

(a) that an application form has been issued;
(b) whether it relates to the exercise of the court's jurisdiction in relation to P's property and affairs, or his personal welfare, or to both; and
(c) of the order or orders sought.

(2) Notification of the issue of the application form must be accompanied by a form for acknowledging notification.

(3) The applicant must file a certificate of notification within 7 days beginning with the date on which notification was given.

Amendments—Word in italics revoked and word in square brackets inserted with effect from 1 July 2015 by virtue of SI 2015/548 (subject to transitional provisions).

71 Requirements for certain applications

A practice direction may make additional or different provision in relation to specified applications.

Responding to an application

72 Responding to an application

(1) A person who is served with or notified of an application form and who wishes to take part in proceedings must file an acknowledgment of service or notification in accordance with this rule.

(2) The acknowledgment of service or notification must be filed not more than *21*[14] days after the application form was served or notification of the application was given.

(3) The court will serve the acknowledgment of service or notification on the applicant and on any other person who has filed such an acknowledgment.

(4) The acknowledgment of service or notification must –

(a) state whether the person acknowledging service or notification consents to the application;
(b) state whether he opposes the application and, if so, set out the grounds for doing so;
(c) state whether he seeks a different order from that set out in the application form and, if so, set out what that order is;
(d) provide an address for service, which must be within the jurisdiction of the court; and
(e) be signed by him or his legal representative.

(5) Subject to rules 120 and 123 (restriction on filing an expert's report and court's power to restrict expert evidence), [unless the court directs otherwise,]where a person who has been served in accordance with rule 66, 67 or 68 opposes the application or seeks a different order, *the acknowledgment of service must be accompanied by*[that person must within 28 days of such service file] a witness statement containing any evidence upon which that person intends to rely.

(6) In addition to complying with the other requirements of this rule, an acknowledgment of notification filed by a person notified of the application in accordance with rule 67(5), 68(5), 69 or 70 must –

- (a) indicate whether the person wishes to be joined as a party to the proceedings; and
- (b) state the person's interest in the proceedings.

(7) Subject to rules 120 and 123 (restriction on filing an expert's report and court's power to restrict expert evidence), [unless the court directs otherwise,] where a person has been notified in accordance with rule 67(5), 68(5), 69, 70, *the acknowledgment of notification must be accompanied by*[that person must within 28 days of such service file] a witness statement containing any evidence of his interest in the proceedings and, if he opposes the application or seeks a different order, any evidence upon which he intends to rely.

(8) The court will consider whether to join a person mentioned in paragraph (6) as a party to the proceedings and, if it decides to do so, will make an order to that effect.

(9) Where a person who is notified in accordance with rule 67(5), 68(5), 69 or 70 complies with the requirements of this rule, he need not comply with the requirements of rule 75 (application to be joined as a party).

(10) Where a person has filed an acknowledgment of notification in accordance with rule 57 (acknowledgment of notification of permission application) he must still acknowledge service or notification of an issued application form in accordance with this rule.

(11) A practice direction may make provision about responding to applications.

Amendments—Words in italics revoked and words in square brackets inserted with effect from 1 July 2015 by virtue of SI 2015/548 (subject to transitional provisions).

The parties to the proceedings

73 Parties to the proceedings

(1) Unless the court otherwise directs, the parties to any proceedings are –

- (a) the applicant; and
- (b) any person who is named as a respondent in the application form and who files an acknowledgment of service in respect of the application form.

(2) The court may order a person to be joined as a party if it considers that it is desirable to do so for the purpose of dealing with the application.

(3) The court may at any time direct that any person who is a party to the proceedings is to be removed as a party.

(4) Unless the court orders otherwise, P shall not be named as a respondent to any proceedings.

(5) A party to the proceedings is bound by any order or direction of the court made in the course of those proceedings.

74 Persons to be bound as if parties

(1) The persons mentioned in paragraph (2) shall be bound by any order made or directions given by the court in the same way that a party to the proceedings is so bound.

(2) The persons referred to in paragraph (1) are –

(a) P; and
(b) any person who has been served with or notified of an application form in accordance with these Rules.

75 Application to be joined as a party

(1) Any person with sufficient interest may apply to the court to be joined as a party to the proceedings.

(2) An application to be joined as a party must be made by filing an application notice in accordance with Part 10 which must –

(a) state the full name and address of the person seeking to be joined as a party to the proceedings;
(b) state his interest in the proceedings;
(c) state whether he consents to the application;
(d) state whether he opposes the application and, if so, set out the grounds for doing so;
(e) state whether he proposes that an order different from that set out in the application form should be made and, if so, set out what that order is;
(f) provide an address for service, which must be within the jurisdiction of the court; and
(g) be signed by him or his legal representative.

(3) Subject to rules 120 and 123 (restriction on filing an expert's report and court's power to restrict expert evidence), an application to be joined must be accompanied by –

(a) a witness statement containing evidence of his interest in the proceedings and, if he proposes that an order different from that set out in the application form should be made, the evidence on which he intends to rely; and
(b) a sufficient number of copies of the application notice to enable service of the application on every other party to the proceedings.

(4) The court will serve the application notice and any accompanying documents on all parties to the proceedings.

(5) The court will consider whether to join a person applying under this rule as a party to the proceedings and, if it decides to do so, will make an order to that effect.

76 Applications for removal as a party to proceedings

A person who wishes to be removed as a party to the proceedings must apply to the court for an order to that effect in accordance with Part 10.

PART 10
APPLICATIONS WITHIN PROCEEDINGS

77 Types of applications for which the Part 10 procedure may be used

(1) The Part 10 procedure is the procedure set out in this Part.

(2) The Part 10 procedure may be used if the application is made by any person –

(a) in the course of existing proceedings; or
(b) as provided for in a rule or practice direction.

(3) The court may grant an interim remedy before an application form has been issued only if –

(a) the matter is urgent; or
(b) it is otherwise necessary to do so in the interests of justice.

(4) An application made during the course of existing proceedings includes an application made during appeal proceedings.

[(5) Where the application seeks solely to withdraw an existing application –

(a) the applicant must file a written request for permission setting out succinctly the reasons for the request;
(b) the request must be in an application notice;
(c) the court may permit an application to be made orally at a hearing or in such alternative written form as it thinks fit.

(6) Where the court deals with a written request under paragraph (5) without a hearing, rule 89 applies to any order so made.

(Rule 87A requires the court's permission to withdraw proceedings.)]

Amendments—Words in square brackets inserted with effect from 1 July 2015 by virtue of SI 2015/548 (subject to transitional provisions).

78 Application notice to be filed

(1) Subject to paragraph (5), the applicant must file an application notice to make an application under this Part.

(2) The applicant must, when he files the application notice, file the evidence upon which he relies (unless such evidence has already been filed).

(3) The court will issue the application notice and, if there is to be a hearing, give notice of the date on which the matter is to be heard by the court.

(4) Notice under paragraph (3) must be given to –

(a) the applicant;
(b) anyone who is named as a respondent in the application notice (if not otherwise a party to the proceedings);
(c) every party to the proceedings; and
(d) any other person, as the court may direct.

(5) An applicant may make an application under this Part without filing an application notice if –

(a) this is permitted by any rule or practice direction; or
(b) the court dispenses with the requirement for an application notice.

ORDER NUMBER

PO NYAATP08

BOOK NUMBER

8848313

BAY NUMBER

2255-6

AUTHOR	Unstated
TITLE	Court of Protection Practice 2015

(6) If the applicant makes an application without giving notice, the evidence in support of the application must state why notice has not been given.

79 What an application notice must include

An application notice must state –

(a) what order or direction the applicant is seeking;
(b) briefly, the grounds on which the applicant is seeking the order or direction; and
(c) such other information as may be required by any rule or a practice direction.

80 Service of an application notice

(1) Subject to paragraphs (4) and (5), the applicant must serve a copy of the application notice on –

(a) anyone who is named as a respondent in the application notice (if not otherwise a party to the proceedings);
(b) every party to the proceedings; and
(c) any other person, as the court may direct,

as soon as practicable and in any event within 21 days of the date on which it was issued.

(2) The application notice must be accompanied by a copy of the evidence filed in support.

(3) The applicant must file a certificate of service within 7 days beginning with the date on which the documents were served.

(4) This rule does not require a copy of evidence to be served on a person upon whom it has already been served, but the applicant must in such a case give to that person notice of the evidence upon which he intends to rely.

(5) An application may be made without serving a copy of the application notice if this is permitted by –

(a) a rule;
(b) a practice direction; or
(c) the court.

81 Applications without notice

(1) This rule applies where the court has dealt with an application which was made without notice having been given to any person.

(2) Where the court makes an order, whether granting or dismissing the application, the applicant must, as soon as practicable or within such period as the court may direct, serve the documents mentioned in paragraph (3) on –

(a) anyone named as a respondent in the application notice (if not otherwise a party to the proceedings);
(b) every party to the proceedings; and
(c) any other person, as the court may direct.

(3) The documents referred to in paragraph (2) are –

(a) a copy of the application notice;
(b) the court's order; and
(c) any evidence filed in support of the application.

(Rule 89 provides for reconsideration of orders made without a hearing or without notice to a person.)

[81A Security for costs]

[(1) A respondent to any application may apply for security for the respondent's costs of the proceedings.

(2) An application for security for costs must be supported by written evidence.

(3) Where the court makes an order for security for costs, it must –

(a) determine the amount of security; and
(b) direct –
  (i) the manner in which; and
  (ii) the time within which,

the security must be given.]

Amendments—Provision inserted with effect from 1 July 2015 by virtue of SI 2015/548.

[81B Conditions to be satisfied]

[(1) The court may make an order for security for costs under rule 81A –

(a) if it is satisfied, having regard to all the circumstances of the case, that it is just to make such an order; and
(b) if –
  (i) one or more of the conditions in paragraph (2) applies; or
  (ii) an enactment permits the court to require security for costs.

(2) The conditions are –

(a) the applicant is –
  (i) resident out of the jurisdiction; but
  (ii) not resident in a Brussels Contracting State, a State bound by the Lugano Convention or a Regulation State, as defined in section 1(3) of the Civil Jurisdiction and Judgments Act 1982;
(b) the applicant is a company or other body (whether incorporated inside or outside Great Britain) and there is reason to believe that it will be unable to pay the respondent's costs if ordered to do so;
(c) the applicant has changed address since proceedings were commenced with a view to avoiding the consequences of the litigation;
(d) the applicant failed to give an address, or gave an incorrect address, in the application form commencing the proceedings;
(e) the applicant is acting as a nominal applicant and there is reason to believe that the applicant will be unable to pay the respondent's costs if ordered to do so;
(f) the applicant has taken steps in relation to the applicant's assets that would make it difficult to enforce an order for costs against the applicant.]

Amendments—Provision inserted with effect from 1 July 2015 by virtue of SI 2015/548.

[81C Security for costs other than from the applicant]

[(1) The respondent may seek an order against a person other than the applicant, and the court may make an order for security for costs against that person, if –

(a) it is satisfied, having regard to all the circumstances of the case, that it is just to make such an order; and
(b) one or more of the conditions in paragraph (2) applies.

(2) The conditions are that the person –

(a) has assigned the right to the substantive matter to the applicant with a view to avoiding the possibility of a costs order being made against the person; or
(b) has contributed or agreed to contribute to the applicant's costs in return for a share of any money or property which the applicant may recover or be awarded in the proceedings; and

is a person against whom a costs order may be made.

(Rule 166 makes provision about costs orders against non-parties.)]

Amendments—Provision inserted with effect from 1 July 2015 by virtue of SI 2015/548.

[81D Security for costs of an appeal]

[(1) The court may order security for costs of an appeal against –

(a) an appellant;
(b) a respondent who also appeals,

on the same grounds as it may order security for costs against an applicant under rule 81A.

(2) The court may also make an order under paragraph (1) where the appellant or the respondent who also appeals is a limited company and there is reason to believe it will be unable to pay the costs of the other parties to the appeal should its appeal be unsuccessful.]

Amendments—Provision inserted with effect from 1 July 2015 by virtue of SI 2015/548.

Interim Remedies

82 Orders for interim remedies

(1) The court may grant the following interim remedies –

(a) an interim injunction;
(b) an interim declaration; or
(c) any other interim order it considers appropriate.

(2) Unless the court orders otherwise, a person on whom an application form is served under Part 9, or who is given notice of such an application, may not apply for an interim remedy before he has filed an acknowledgment of service or notification in accordance with Part 9.

(3) This rule does not limit any other power of the court to grant interim relief.

PART 10A
DEPRIVATION OF LIBERTY

82A The practice direction to this Part sets out procedure governing –

(a) applications to the court for orders relating to the deprivation, or proposed deprivation, of liberty of P; and
(b) proceedings (for example, relating to costs or appeals) connected with or consequent upon such applications.

PART 11
HUMAN RIGHTS

83 General

(1) A party who seeks to rely upon any provision of or right arising under the Human Rights Act 1998 ('the 1998 Act') or who seeks a remedy available under that Act must inform the court in the manner set out in the relevant practice direction specifying –

(a) the Convention right (within the meaning of the 1998 Act) which it is alleged has been infringed and details of the alleged infringement; and
(b) the remedy sought and whether this includes a declaration of incompatibility under section 4 of the 1998 Act.

(2) The court may not make a declaration of incompatibility unless 21 days' notice, or such other period of notice as the court directs, has been given to the Crown.

(3) Where notice has been given to the Crown, a Minister or other person permitted by the 1998 Act will be joined as a party on filing an application in accordance with rule 75 (application to be joined as a party).

PART 12
DEALING WITH APPLICATIONS

84 Dealing with the application

(1) As soon as practicable after any application has been issued the court shall consider how to deal with it.

[(1A) Where permission to start proceedings is required, and whether or not it has been applied for, the court's consideration under paragraph (1) shall include whether to grant or refuse permission without a hearing, or to direct a hearing to consider whether permission should be granted.]

(2) The court may deal with an application or any part of an application at a hearing or without a hearing.

(3) In considering whether it is necessary to hold a hearing, the court shall, as appropriate, have regard to –

(a) the nature of the proceedings and the orders sought;
(b) whether the application is opposed by a person who appears to the court to have an interest in matters relating to P's best interests;
(c) whether the application involves a substantial dispute of fact;
(d) the complexity of the facts and the law;
(e) any wider public interest in the proceedings;

(f) the circumstances of P and of any party, in particular as to whether their rights would be adequately protected if a hearing were not held;
(g) whether the parties agree that the court should dispose of the application without a hearing; and
(h) any other matter specified in the relevant practice direction.

(4) Where the court considers that a hearing is necessary, it will –

(a) give notice of the hearing date to the parties and to any other person it directs; and
(b) state *whether the hearing is for disposing of the matter or for directions*[what is to be dealt with at the hearing, including whether the matter is to be disposed of at that hearing].

(5) Where the court decides that it can deal with the matter without a hearing it will do so and serve a copy of its order on the parties and on any other person it directs.

Amendments—Words in italics revoked and words in square brackets inserted with effect from 1 July 2015 by virtue of SI 2015/548.

85 Directions

(1) The court may –

(a) give directions in writing; or
(b) set a date for a directions hearing; and
(c) do anything else that may be set out in a practice direction.

(2) When giving directions, the court may do any of the following –

(a) require a report under section 49 of the Act and give directions as to any such report;
(b) give directions as to any requirements contained in these Rules or a practice direction for the giving of notification to any person or for that person to do anything in response to a notification;
(c) if the court considers that P should be a party to the proceedings, give directions joining him as a party;
(d) if P is joined as a party to proceedings, give directions as to the appointment of a litigation friend;
(e) if the court considers that any other person or persons should be a party to the proceedings, give directions joining them as a party;
(f) if the court considers that any party to the proceedings should not be a party, give directions for that person's removal as a party;
(g) give directions for the management of the case and set a timetable for the steps to be taken between the giving of directions and the hearing;
(h) subject to rule 86, give directions as to the type of judge who is to hear the case;
(i) give directions as to whether the proceedings or any part of them are to be heard in public, or as to whether any particular person should be permitted to attend the hearing, or as to whether any publication of the proceedings is to be permitted;
(j) give directions as to the disclosure of documents, service of witness statements and any expert evidence;
(k) give directions as to the attendance of witnesses and as to whether, and the extent to which, cross-examination will be permitted at any hearing; and
(l) give such other directions as the court thinks fit.

(3) The court may give directions at any time –

(a) on its own initiative; or
(b) on the application of a party.

(4) Subject to paragraphs (5) and (6) and unless these Rules or a practice direction provide otherwise or the court directs otherwise, the time specified by a rule or by the court for a person to do any act may be varied by the written agreement of the parties.

(5) A party must apply to the court if he wishes to vary –

(a) the date the court has fixed for the final hearing; or
(b) the period within which the final hearing is to take place.

(6) The time specified by a rule or practice direction or by the court may not be varied by the parties if the variation would make it necessary to vary the date the court has fixed for any hearing or the period within which the final hearing is to take place.

[(Participation of P in proceedings is addressed in rule 3A (participation of P) and Part 17 (litigation friends and rule 3A representatives).)]

Amendments—Words in italics revoked and words in square brackets inserted with effect from 1 July 2015 by virtue of SI 2015/548.

Allocation of proceedings

86 Court's jurisdiction in certain kinds of case to be exercised by certain judges

(1) The court will consider whether the application is of a type specified in the relevant Practice Direction as being one which must be dealt with by –

(a) the President;
(b) the Vice-President; or
(c) one of the other judges nominated by virtue of section 46(2)(a) to (c) of the Act.

(2) The practice direction made under this rule shall specify the categories of case which must be dealt with by a judge mentioned in paragraph (1).

(3) Applications in any matter other than those specified in the relevant practice direction may be dealt with by any judge.

[86 Court's jurisdiction in certain kinds of case to be exercised by certain judges]

[(1) A practice direction made under this rule may specify certain categories of case to be dealt with by a specific judge or a specific class of judges.

(2) Applications in any matter other than those specified in the practice direction referred to in paragraph (1) may be dealt with by any judge.]

Amendments—Provision substituted with effect from 6 April 2015 by virtue of SI 2015/548.

Disputing the jurisdiction of the court

87 Procedure for disputing the court's jurisdiction

(1) A person who wishes to –

(a) dispute the court's jurisdiction to hear an application; or
(b) argue that the court should not exercise its jurisdiction,

may apply to the court at any time for an order declaring that it has no such jurisdiction or should not exercise any jurisdiction that it may have.

(2) An application under this rule must be –

(a) made by using the form specified in the relevant practice direction; and
(b) supported by evidence.

(3) An order containing a declaration that the court has no jurisdiction or will not exercise its jurisdiction may also make further provision, including –

(a) setting aside the application;
(b) discharging any order made; *and*
(c) staying the proceedings.[;
(d) discharging any litigation friend, accredited legal representative or representative.]

Amendments—Word in italics revoked and words in square brackets inserted with effect from 1 July 2015 by virtue of SI 2015/548.

[87A Permission required to withdraw proceedings]

[(1) Proceedings may only be withdrawn with the permission of the court.

(2) An application to withdraw proceedings must be made in accordance with Part 10.]

Amendments—Provision inserted with effect from 1 July 2015 by virtue of SI 2015/548 (subject to transitional provisions).

Participation in hearings

88 Participation in hearings

(1) The court may hear P on the question of whether or not an order should be made, whether or not he is a party to the proceedings.

(2) The court may proceed with a hearing in the absence of P if it considers that it would be appropriate to do so.

(3) A person other than P who is served with or notified of the application may only take part in a hearing if –

(a) he files an acknowledgment in accordance with the Rules and is made a party to the proceedings; or
(b) the court permits.

[(Rule 3A deals with participation of P.)]

Amendments—Words in square brackets inserted with effect from 1 July 2015 by virtue of SI 2015/548.

Reconsideration of court orders

89 Orders made without a hearing or without notice to any person

(1) This rule applies where the court makes an order –

(a) without a hearing; or
(b) without notice to any person who is affected by it.

(2) Where this rule applies –

(a) P;
(b) any party to the proceedings; or
(c) any other person affected by the order,

may apply to the court for reconsideration of the order made.

(3) An application under paragraph (2) must be made –

(a) within 21 days of the order being served or such other period as the court may direct; and
(b) in accordance with Part 10.

(4) The court will –

(a) reconsider the order without directing a hearing; or
(b) fix a date for the matter to be heard, and notify all parties to the proceedings and such other persons as the court may direct, of that date.

(5) Where an application is made in accordance with this rule, the court may affirm, set aside or vary any order made.

(6) Reconsideration may be by any judge of the court –

(a) including the judge who made the decision in respect of which the reconsideration is sought; but
(b) may not be by a judge who is not a prescribed higher judge within the meaning of section 53(3) of the Act in relation to the first-mentioned judge.

[(6) An order made by a court officer authorised under rule 7A may be reconsidered by any judge.

(6A) An order made by a Tier 1 Judge may be reconsidered by any judge.

(6B) An order made by a Tier 2 Judge may be reconsidered by any Tier 2 Judge or by a Tier 3 Judge.

(6C) An order made by a Tier 3 Judge may be reconsidered by any Tier 3 Judge.

(6D) In any case to which paragraphs (6A) to (6C) apply the reconsideration may be carried out by the judge who made the order being reconsidered.]

(7) No application may be made seeking a reconsideration of a decision that has been made under paragraph (5).

[(7) No application may be made seeking a reconsideration of –

(a) an order that has been made under paragraph (5); or
(b) an order granting or refusing permission to appeal.]

(8) An appeal against *a decision*[an order] made under paragraph (5) may be made in accordance with Part 20 (appeals).

(9) Any order made without a hearing or without notice to any person, other than one made under paragraph (5) [or one granting or refusing permission to appeal], must contain a statement of the right to apply for a reconsideration of the decision in accordance with this rule.

(10) An application made under this rule may include a request that the court reconsider the matter at a hearing.

[(Rule 7A(2)(c) provides that a court officer authorised under that rule may not deal with an application for the reconsideration of an order made by that court officer or another court officer.)]

Amendments—Words in italics revoked and words in square brackets inserted with effect from 6 April 2015 by virtue of SI 2015/548 (subject to transitional provisions).

PART 13
HEARINGS

Private hearings

90 General rule – hearing to be in private

(1) The general rule is that a hearing is to be held in private.

(2) A private hearing is a hearing which only the following persons are entitled to attend –

(a) the parties;
(b) P (whether or not a party);
(c) any person acting in the proceedings as a litigation friend;
(d) any legal representative of a person specified in any of sub-paragraphs (a) to (c); and
(e) any court officer.

(3) In relation to a private hearing, the court may make an order –

(a) authorising any person, or class of persons, to attend the hearing or a part of it; or
(b) excluding any person, or class of persons, from attending the hearing or a part of it.

91 Court's general power to authorise publication of information about proceedings

(1) For the purposes of the law relating to contempt of court, information relating to proceedings held in private *may be published where the court makes an order under paragraph (2)*[(whether or not contained in a document filed with the court) may be communicated in accordance with paragraph (2) or (2A)].

(2) The court may make an order authorising –

(a) the publication [or communication] of such information [or material] relating to the proceedings as it may specify; or
(b) the publication of the text or a summary of the whole or part of a judgment or order made by the court.

[(2A) Subject to any direction of the court, information referred to in paragraph (1) may be communicated in accordance with Practice Direction 13A.]

(3) Where the court makes an order under paragraph (2) it may do so on such terms as it thinks fit, and in particular may –

- (a) impose restrictions on the publication of the identity of –
  - (i) any party;
  - (ii) P (whether or not a party);
  - (iii) any witness; or
  - (iv) any other person;
- (b) prohibit the publication of any information that may lead to any such person being identified;
- (c) prohibit the further publication of any information relating to the proceedings from such date as the court may specify; or
- (d) impose such other restrictions on the publication of information relating to the proceedings as the court may specify.

[(4) The court may on its own initiative or upon request authorise communication –

- (a) for the purposes set out in Practice Direction 13A; or
- (b) for such other purposes as it considers appropriate,

of information held by it.]

Amendments—Words in italics revoked and words in square brackets inserted with effect from 1 July 2015 by virtue of SI 2015/548.

__Power to order a public hearing__

92 Court's power to order that a hearing be held in public

(1) The court may make an order –

- (a) for a hearing to be held in public;
- (b) for a part of a hearing to be held in public; or
- (c) excluding any person, or class of persons, from attending a public hearing or a part of it.

(2) Where the court makes an order under paragraph (1), it may in the same order or by a subsequent order –

- (a) impose restrictions on the publication of the identity of –
  - (i) any party;
  - (ii) P (whether or not a party);
  - (iii) any witness; or
  - (iv) any other person;
- (b) prohibit the publication of any information that may lead to any such person being identified;
- (c) prohibit the further publication of any information relating to the proceedings from such date as the court may specify; or
- (d) impose such other restrictions on the publication of information relating to the proceedings as the court may specify.

__Supplementary__

93 Supplementary provisions relating to public or private hearings

(1) An order under rule 90, 91 or 92 may be made –

(a) only where it appears to the court that there is good reason for making the order;
(b) at any time; and
(c) either on the court's own initiative or on an application made by any person in accordance with Part 10.

(2) A practice direction may make further provision in connection with –

(a) private hearings;
(b) public hearings; or
(c) the publication of information about any proceedings.

PART 14
ADMISSIONS, EVIDENCE AND DEPOSITIONS

Admissions

94 Making an admission

(1) Without prejudice to the ability to make an admission in any other way, a party may admit the truth of the whole or part of another party's case by giving notice in writing.

(2) The court may allow a party to amend or withdraw an admission.

Evidence

95 Power of court to control evidence

The court may –

(a) control the evidence by giving directions as to –
   (i) the issues on which it requires evidence;
   (ii) the nature of the evidence which it requires to decide those issues; and
   (iii) the way in which the evidence is to be placed before the court;
(b) use its power under this rule to exclude evidence that would otherwise be admissible;
(c) allow or limit cross-examination; *and*
(d) admit such evidence, whether written or oral, as it thinks fit.
[(d) admit such evidence, whether written or oral, as it thinks fit; and
(e) admit, accept and act upon such information, whether oral or written, from P, any protected party or any person who lacks competence to give evidence, as the court considers sufficient, although not given on oath and whether or not it would be admissible in a court of law apart from this rule.]

Amendments—Words in italics revoked and words in square brackets inserted with effect from 1 July 2015 by virtue of SI 2015/548.

96 Evidence of witnesses – general rule

(1) The general rule is that any fact which needs to be proved by evidence of a witness is to be proved –

(a) where there is a final hearing, by their oral evidence; or
(b) at any other hearing, or if there is no hearing, by their evidence in writing.

(2) Where a witness is called to give oral evidence under paragraph (1)(a), his witness statement shall stand as his evidence in chief unless the court directs otherwise.

(3) A witness giving oral evidence at the final hearing may, if the court permits –

(a) amplify his witness statement; and
(b) give evidence in relation to new matters which have arisen since the witness statement was made.

(4) The court may so permit only if it considers that there is good reason not to confine the evidence of the witness to the contents of his witness statement.

(5) This rule is subject to –

(a) any provision to the contrary in these Rules or elsewhere; or
(b) any order or direction of the court.

97 Written evidence – general rule

A party may not rely upon written evidence unless –

(a) it has been filed in accordance with these Rules or a practice direction;
(b) it is expressly permitted by these Rules or a practice direction; or
(c) the court gives permission.

98 Evidence by video link or other means

The court may allow a witness to give evidence through a video link or by other communication technology.

99 Service of witness statements for use at final hearing

(1) A witness statement is a written statement which contains the evidence which that person would be allowed to give orally.

(2) The court will give directions about the service of any witness statement that a party intends to rely upon at the final hearing.

(3) The court may give directions as to the order in which witness statements are to be served.

(Rules 11 and 100 require witness statements to be verified by a statement of truth.)

100 Form of witness statement

A witness statement must contain a statement of truth and comply with the requirements set out in the relevant practice direction.

101 Witness summaries

(1) A party who wishes to file a witness statement for use at final hearing, but is unable to do so, may apply, without notice, to be permitted to file a witness summary instead.

(2) A witness summary is a summary of –

(a) the evidence, if known, which would otherwise be included in a witness statement; or
(b) if the evidence is not known, the matters about which the party filing the witness summary proposes to question the witness.

(3) Unless the court directs otherwise, a witness summary must include the name and address of the intended witness.

(4) Unless the court directs otherwise, a witness summary must be filed within the period in which a witness statement would have had to be filed.

(5) Where a party files a witness summary, so far as practicable, rules 96(3)(a) (amplifying witness statements) and 99 (service of witness statements for use at a final hearing) shall apply to the summary.

102 Affidavit evidence

Evidence must be given by affidavit instead of or in addition to a witness statement if this is required by the court, a provision contained in any rule, a practice direction or any other enactment.

103 Form of affidavit

An affidavit must comply with the requirements set out in the relevant practice direction.

104 Affidavit made outside the jurisdiction

A person may make an affidavit outside the jurisdiction in accordance with –

(a) this Part; or
(b) the law of the place where he makes the affidavit.

105 Notarial acts and instruments

A notarial act or instrument may, without further proof, be received in evidence as duly authenticated in accordance with the requirements of law unless the contrary is proved.

106 Summoning of witnesses

(1) The court may allow or direct any party to issue a witness summons requiring the person named in it to attend before the court and give oral evidence or produce any document to the court.

(2) An application by a party for the issue of a witness summons may be made by filing an application notice which includes –

(a) the name and address of the applicant and of his solicitor, if any;
(b) the name, address and occupation of the proposed witness;
(c) particulars of any document which the proposed witness is to be required to produce; and

(d) the grounds on which the application is made.

(3) The general rule is that a witness summons is binding if it is served at least 7 days before the date on which the witness is required to attend before the court, and the requirements of paragraph (6) have been complied with.

(4) The court may direct that a witness summons shall be binding although it will be served less than 7 days before the date on which the witness is required to attend before the court.

(5) Unless the court directs otherwise, a witness summons is to be served by the person making the application.

(6) At the time of service the witness must be offered or paid –

(a) a sum reasonably sufficient to cover his expenses in travelling to and from the court; and
(b) such sum by way of compensation for loss of time as may be specified in the relevant practice direction.

(7) The court may order that the witness is to be paid such general costs as it considers appropriate.

107 Power of court to direct a party to provide information

(1) Where a party has access to information which is not reasonably available to the other party, the court may direct that party to prepare and file a document recording the information.

(2) The court will give directions about serving a copy of that document on the other parties.

Depositions

108 Evidence by deposition

(1) A party may apply for an order for a person to be examined before the hearing takes place.

(2) A person from whom evidence is to be obtained following an order under this rule is referred to as a 'deponent' and the evidence is referred to as a 'deposition'.

(3) An order under this rule shall be for a deponent to be examined on oath before –

(a) a circuit judge or a district judge, whether or not nominated as a judge of the court;
(b) an examiner of the court; or
(c) such other person as the court appoints.

(4) The order may require the production of any document which the court considers is necessary for the purposes of the examination.

(5) The order will state the date, time and place of the examination.

(6) At the time of service of the order, the deponent must be offered or paid –

(a) a sum reasonably sufficient to cover his expenses in travelling to and from the place of examination; and
(b) such sum by way of compensation for loss of time as may be specified in the relevant practice direction.

(7) Where the court makes an order for a deposition to be taken, it may also order the party who obtained the order to file a witness statement or witness summary in relation to the evidence to be given by the person to be examined.

109 Conduct of examination

(1) Subject to any directions contained in the order for examination, the examination must be conducted in the same way as if the witness were giving evidence at a final hearing.

(2) If all the parties are present, the examiner may conduct the examination of a person not named in the order for examination if all the parties and the person to be examined consent.

(3) The examiner must ensure that the evidence given by the witness is recorded in full.

(4) The examiner must send a copy of the deposition –

(a) to the person who obtained the order for the examination of the witness; and

(b) to the court.

(5) The court will give directions as to the service of a copy of the deposition on the other parties.

110 Fees and expenses of examiners of the court

(1) An examiner of the court may charge a fee for the examination and he need not send the deposition to the court until the fee is paid, unless the court directs otherwise.

(2) The examiner's fees and expenses must be paid by the party who obtained the order for examination.

(3) If the fees and expenses due to an examiner are not paid within a reasonable time, he may report that fact to the court.

(4) The court may order the party who obtained the order for examination to deposit in the court office a specified sum in respect of the examiner's fees and, where it does so, the examiner will not be asked to act until the sum has been deposited.

(5) An order under this rule does not affect any decision as to the person who is ultimately to bear the costs of the examination.

111 Examiners of the court

(1) The Lord Chancellor shall appoint persons to be examiners of the court.

(2) The persons appointed shall be barristers or solicitor-advocates who have been practising for a period of not less than 3 years.

(3) The Lord Chancellor may revoke an appointment at any time.

(4) In addition to appointing persons in accordance with this rule, examiners appointed under rule 34.15 of the Civil Procedure Rules 1998 may act as examiners in the court.

112 Enforcing attendance of a witness

(1) If a person served with an order to attend before an examiner –

(a) fails to attend; or
(b) refuses to be sworn for the purpose of the examination or to answer any lawful question or produce any document at the examination,

a certificate of his failure or refusal, signed by the examiner, must be filed by the party requiring the deposition.

(2) On the certificate being filed, the party requiring the deposition may apply to the court for an order requiring that person to attend or to be sworn or to answer any question or produce any document, as the case may be.

(3) An application for an order under this rule may be made without notice.

(4) The court may order the person against whom an order is sought or made under this rule to pay any costs resulting from his failure or refusal.

113 Use of deposition at a hearing

(1) A deposition ordered under rule 108, 115 or 116 may be put in evidence at a hearing unless the court orders otherwise.

(2) A party intending to put a deposition in evidence at a hearing must file notice of his intention to do so on the court and serve the notice on every other party.

(3) Unless the court directs otherwise, he must file the notice at least 14 days before the day fixed for the hearing.

(4) The court may require a deponent to attend the hearing and give evidence orally.

Taking evidence outside the jurisdiction

114 Interpretation

In this Section –

(a) 'Regulation State' has the same meaning as 'Member State' in the Taking of Evidence Regulation, that is all Member States except Denmark; and
(b) 'the Taking of Evidence Regulation' means Council Regulation (EC) No. 1206/2001 of 28 May 2001 on co-operation between the courts of Member States in the taking of evidence in civil and commercial matters.

115 Where a person to be examined is in another Regulation State

(1) This rule applies where a party wishes to take a deposition from a person who is –

(a) outside the jurisdiction; and
(b) in a Regulation State.

(2) The court may order the issue of the request to a designated court ('the requested court') in the Regulation State in which the proposed deponent is.

(3) If the court makes an order for the issue of a request, the party who sought the order must file –

(a) a draft Form A as set out in the annex to the Taking of Evidence Regulation (request for the taking of evidence);
(b) except where paragraph (4) applies, a translation of the form;
(c) an undertaking to be responsible for the costs sought by the requested court in relation to –
  (i) fees paid to experts and interpreters; and
  (ii) where requested by that party, the use of special procedure or communications technology; and
(d) an undertaking to be responsible for the court's expenses.

(4) There is no need to file a translation if –

(a) English is one of the official languages of the Regulation State where the examination is to take place; or
(b) the Regulation State has indicated, in accordance with the Taking of Evidence Regulation, that English is a language which it will accept.

(5) Where article 17 of the Taking of Evidence Regulation (direct taking of evidence by the requested court) allows evidence to be taken directly in another Regulation State, the court may make an order for the submission of a request in accordance with that article.

(6) If the court makes an order for the submission of a request under paragraph (5), the party who sought the order must file –

(a) draft Form I as set out in the annex to the Taking of Evidence Regulation (request for direct taking of evidence);
(b) except where paragraph (4) applies, a translation of the form; and
(c) an undertaking to be responsible for the requested court's expenses.

116 Where a person to be examined is out of the jurisdiction – letter of request

(1) This rule applies where a party wishes to take a deposition from a person who is –

(a) out of the jurisdiction; and
(b) not in a Regulation State within the meaning of rule 114.

(2) The court may order the issue of a letter of request to the judicial authorities of the country in which the proposed deponent is.

(3) A letter of request is a request to a judicial authority to take the evidence of that person, or arrange for it to be taken.

(4) If the government of a country permits a person appointed by the court to examine a person in that country, the court may make an order appointing a special examiner for that purpose.

(5) A person may be examined under this rule on oath or affirmation in accordance with any procedure permitted in the country in which the examination is to take place.

(6) If the court makes an order for the issue of a letter of request, the party who sought the order must file –

(a) the following documents and, except where paragraph (7) applies, a translation of them –
  (i) a draft letter of request;

(ii) a statement of the issues relevant to the proceedings; and
(iii) a list of questions or the subject matter of questions to be put to the person to be examined; and

(b) an undertaking to be responsible for the Secretary of State's expenses.

(7) There is no need to file a translation if –

(a) English is one of the official languages of the country where the examination is to take place; or
(b) a practice direction has specified that country is a country where no translation is necessary.

Section 49 reports

117 Reports under section 49 of the Act

(1) This rule applies where the court requires a report to be made to it under section 49 of the Act.

(2) It is the duty of the person who is required to make the report to help the court on the matters within his expertise.

(3) Unless the court directs otherwise, the person making the report must –

(a) contact or seek to interview such persons as he thinks appropriate or as the court directs;
(b) to the extent that it is practicable and appropriate to do so, ascertain what P's wishes and feelings are, and the beliefs and values that would be likely to influence P if he had the capacity to make a decision in relation to the matter to which the application relates;
(c) describe P's circumstances; and
(d) address such other matters as are required in a practice direction or as the court may direct.

(4) The court will send a copy of the report to the parties and to such persons as the court may direct.

(5) Subject to paragraphs (6) and (7), the person who is required to make the report may examine and take copies of any document in the court records.

(6) The court may direct that the right to inspect documents under this rule does not apply in relation to such documents, or descriptions of documents, as the court may specify.

(7) The court may direct that any information is to be provided to the maker of the report on an edited basis.

118 Written questions to person making a report under section 49

(1) Where a report is made under section 49 the court may, on the application of any party, permit written questions relevant to the issues before the court to be put to the person by whom the report was made.

(2) The questions sought to be put to the maker of the report shall be submitted to the court, and the court may put them to the maker of the report with such amendments (if any) as it thinks fit and the maker of the report shall give his replies in writing to the questions so put.

(3) The court will send a copy of the replies given by the maker of the report under this rule to the parties and to such other persons as the court may direct.

PART 15
EXPERTS

119 References to expert

A reference to an expert in this Part –

(a) is to an expert who has been instructed to give or prepare evidence for the purpose of court proceedings; but
(b) does not include any person instructed to make a report under section 49 of the Act.

120 Restriction on filing an expert's report

(1) No person may file expert evidence unless the court or a practice direction permits, or if it is filed with the *permission form or* application form and is evidence –

(a) that P is a person who lacks capacity to make a decision or decisions in relation to the matter or matters to which the application relates;
(b) as to P's best interests; or
(c) that is required by any rule or practice direction to be filed with the *permission form or* application form.

(2) An applicant may only rely upon any expert evidence so filed in support of the *permission form or* application form to the extent and for the purposes that the court allows.

(Rule 64(a) requires the applicant to file any evidence upon which he wishes to rely with the application form *and rule 54 requires certain documents to be filed with the application for permission form.*)

Amendments—Words in italics revoked with effect from 1 July 2015 by virtue of SI 2015/548 (subject to transitional provisions).

121 Duty to restrict expert evidence

Expert evidence shall be restricted to that which is reasonably required to resolve the proceedings.

122 Experts – overriding duty to the court

It is the duty of the expert to help the court on the matters within his expertise.

123 Court's power to restrict expert evidence

(1) Subject to rule 120, no party may file or adduce expert evidence unless the court or a practice direction permits.

(2) When a party applies for a direction under this rule he must –

(a) identify the field in respect of which he wishes to rely upon expert evidence;
(b) where practicable, identify the expert in that field upon whose evidence he wishes to rely;
(c) provide any other material information about the expert; and
(d) provide a draft letter of instruction to the expert.

(3) Where a direction is given under this rule, the court shall specify the field or fields in respect of which the expert evidence is to be provided.

(4) The court may specify the person who is to provide the evidence referred to in paragraph (3).

(5) Where a direction is given under this rule for a party to call an expert or put in evidence an expert's report, the court shall give directions for the service of the report on the parties and on such other persons as the court may direct.

(6) The court may limit the amount of the expert's fees and expenses that the party who wishes to rely upon the expert may recover from any other party.

124 General requirement for expert evidence to be given in a written report

Expert evidence is to be given in a written report unless the court directs otherwise.

125 Written questions to experts

(1) A party may put written questions to –

(a) an expert instructed by another party; or
(b) a single joint expert appointed under rule 130,

about a report prepared by such person.

(2) Written questions under paragraph (1) –

(a) may be put once only;
(b) must be put within 28 days beginning with the date on which the expert's report was served; and
(c) must be for the purpose only of clarification of the report.

(3) Paragraph (2) does not apply in any case where –

(a) the court permits it to be done on a further occasion;
(b) the other party or parties agree; or
(c) any practice direction provides otherwise.

(4) An expert's answers to questions put in accordance with paragraph (1) shall be treated as part of the expert's report.

(5) Paragraph (6) applies where –

(a) a party has put a written question to an expert instructed by another party in accordance with this rule; and
(b) the expert does not answer that question.

(6) The court may make one or both of the following orders in relation to the party who instructed the expert –

(a) that the party may not rely upon the evidence of that expert; or

(b) that the party may not recover the fees and expenses of that expert, or part of them, from any other party.

(7) Unless the court otherwise directs, and subject to any final costs order that may be made, the instructing party is responsible for the payment of the expert's fees and expenses, including the expert's costs of answering questions put by any other party.

126 Contents of expert's report

(1) The court may give directions as to the matters to be covered in an expert's report.

(2) An expert's report must comply with the requirements set out in the relevant practice direction.

(3) At the end of an expert's report there must be a statement that –

(a) the expert understands his duty to the court; and
(b) he has complied with that duty.

(4) The expert's report must state the substance of all material instructions, whether written or oral, on the basis of which the report was written.

(5) The instructions to the expert shall not be privileged against disclosure.

127 Use by one party of expert's report disclosed by another

Where a party has disclosed an expert's report, any party may use that expert's report as evidence at any hearing in the proceedings.

128 Discussions between experts

(1) The court may, at any stage, direct a discussion between experts for the purpose of requiring the experts to –

(a) identify and discuss the expert issues in the proceedings; and
(b) where possible, reach an agreed opinion on those issues.

(2) The court may specify the issues which the experts must discuss.

(3) The court may direct that following a discussion between the experts they must prepare a statement for the court showing –

(a) those issues on which they agree; and
(b) those issues on which they disagree and a summary of their reasons for disagreeing.

(4) Unless the court otherwise directs, the content of the discussions between experts may be referred to at any hearing or at any stage in the proceedings.

129 Expert's right to ask court for directions

(1) An expert may file a written request for directions to assist him in carrying out his function as an expert.

(2) An expert must, unless the court directs otherwise, provide a copy of any proposed request for directions under paragraph (1) –

(a) to the party instructing him, at least 7 days before he files the request; and
(b) to all other parties, at least 4 days before he files it.

(3) The court, when it gives directions, may also direct that a party be served with a copy of the directions.

130 Court's power to direct that evidence is to be given by a single joint expert

(1) Where two or more parties wish to submit expert evidence on a particular issue, the court may direct that the evidence on that issue is to be given by one expert only.

(2) The parties wishing to submit the expert evidence are called 'the instructing parties'.

(3) Where the instructing parties cannot agree who should be the expert, the court may –

(a) select the expert from a list prepared or identified by the instructing parties; or
(b) direct the manner by which the expert is to be selected.

131 Instructions to a single joint expert

(1) Where the court gives a direction under rule 130 for a single joint expert to be used, each party may give instructions to the expert.

(2) Unless the court otherwise directs, when an instructing party gives instructions to the expert he must, at the same time, send a copy of the instructions to the other instructing parties.

(3) The court may give directions about –

(a) the payment of the expert's fees and expenses; and
(b) any inspection, examination or experiments which the expert wishes to carry out.

(4) The court may, before an expert is instructed, limit the amount that can be paid by way of fees and expenses to the expert.

(5) Unless the court otherwise directs, and subject to any final costs order that may be made, the instructing parties are jointly and severally liable for the payment of the expert's fees and expenses.

PART 16
DISCLOSURE

132 Meaning of disclosure

A party discloses a document by stating that the document exists or has existed.

133 General or specific disclosure

(1) The court may either on its own initiative or on the application of a party make an order to give general or specific disclosure.

(2) General disclosure requires a party to disclose –

(a) the documents on which he relies; and
(b) the documents which –
  (i) adversely affect his own case;
  (ii) adversely affect another party's case; or
  (iii) support another party's case.

(3) An order for specific disclosure is an order that a party must do one or more of the following things –

(a) disclose documents or classes of documents specified in the order;
(b) carry out a search to the extent stated in the order; or
(c) disclose any document located as a result of that search.

(4) A party's duty to disclose documents is limited to documents which are or have been in his control.

(5) For the purpose of paragraph (4) a party has or has had a document in his control if –

(a) it is or was in his physical possession;
(b) he has or has had possession of it; or
(c) he has or has had a right to inspect or take copies of it.

134 Procedure for general or specific disclosure

(1) This rule applies where the court makes an order under rule 133 to give general or specific disclosure.

(2) Each party must make, and serve on every other party, a list of documents to be disclosed.

(3) A copy of each list must be filed within 7 days of the date on which it is served.

(4) The list must identify the documents in a convenient order and manner and as concisely as possible.

(5) The list must indicate –

(a) the documents in respect of which the party claims a right or duty to withhold inspection (see rule 138); and
(b) the documents that are no longer in his control, stating what has happened to them.

135 Ongoing duty of disclosure

(1) Where the court makes an order to give general or specific disclosure under rule 133, any party to whom the order applies is under a continuing duty to provide such disclosure as is required by the order until the proceedings are concluded.

(2) If a document to which the duty of disclosure imposed by paragraph (1) extends comes to a party's notice at any time during the proceedings, he must immediately notify every other party.

136 Right to inspect documents

(1) A party to whom a document has been disclosed has a right to inspect any document disclosed to him except where –

(a) the document is no longer in the control of the party who disclosed it; or
(b) the party disclosing the document has a right or duty to withhold inspection of it.

(2) The right to inspect disclosed documents extends to any document mentioned in –

(a) a document filed or served in the course of the proceedings by any other party; or
(b) correspondence sent by any other party.

137 Inspection and copying of documents

(1) Where a party has a right to inspect a document, he –

(a) must give the party who disclosed the document written notice of his wish to inspect it; and
(b) may request a copy of the document.

(2) Not more than 14 days after the date on which the party who disclosed the document received the notice under paragraph (1)(a), he must permit inspection of the document at a convenient place and time.

(3) Where a party has requested a copy of the document, the party who disclosed the document must supply him with a copy not more than 14 days after the date on which he received the request.

(4) For the purposes of paragraph (2), the party who disclosed the document must give reasonable notice of the time and place for inspection.

(5) For the purposes of paragraph (3), the party requesting a copy of the document is responsible for the payment of reasonable copying costs, subject to any final costs order that may be made.

138 Claim to withhold inspection or disclosure of document

(1) A party who wishes to claim that he has a right or duty to withhold inspection of a document, or part of a document, must state in writing –

(a) that he has such a right or duty; and
(b) the grounds on which he claims that right or duty.

(2) The statement must be made in the list in which the document is disclosed (see rule 134(2)).

(3) A party may, by filing an application notice in accordance with Part 10, apply to the court to decide whether the claim made under paragraph (1) should be upheld.

139 Consequence of failure to disclose documents or permit inspection

A party may not rely upon any document which he fails to disclose or in respect of which he fails to permit inspection unless the court permits.

PART 17
LITIGATION FRIEND

140 Who may act as a litigation friend

(1) A person may act as a litigation friend on behalf of a person mentioned in paragraph (2) if he –

- *(a) can fairly and competently conduct proceedings on behalf of that person; and*
- *(b) has no interests adverse to those of that person.*

(2) The persons for whom a litigation friend may act are –

- *(a) P;*
- *(b) a child; or*
- *(c) a protected party.*

141 Requirement for a litigation friend

(1) Subject to rule 147, P (if a party to proceedings) must have a litigation friend.

(2) A protected party (if a party to the proceedings) must have a litigation friend.

(3) A child (if a party to proceedings) must have a litigation friend to conduct those proceedings on his behalf unless the court makes an order under paragraph (4).

(4) The court may make an order permitting the child to conduct proceedings without a litigation friend.

(5) An application for an order under paragraph (4) –

- *(a) may be made by the child;*
- *(b) if the child already has a litigation friend, must be made on notice to the litigation friend; and*
- *(c) if the child has no litigation friend, may be made without notice.*

(6) Where –

- *(a) the court has made an order under paragraph (4); and*
- *(b) it subsequently appears to the court that it is desirable for a litigation friend to conduct the proceedings on behalf of the child,*

the court may appoint a person to be the child's litigation friend.

142 Litigation friend without a court order

(1) This rule does not apply –

- *(a) in relation to P;*
- *(b) where the court has appointed a person under rule 143 or 144; or*
- *(c) where the Official Solicitor is to act as litigation friend.*

(2) A deputy with the power to conduct legal proceedings in the name of the protected party or on the protected party's behalf is entitled to be a litigation friend of the protected party in any proceedings to which his power relates.

(3) If no one has been appointed by the court, or in the case of a protected party, there is no deputy with the power to conduct proceedings, a person who wishes to act as a litigation friend must –

(a) file a certificate of suitability stating that he satisfies the conditions specified in rule 140(1); and
(b) serve the certificate of suitability on –
  (i) the person on whom an application form is to be served in accordance with rule 32 (service on children and protected parties); and
  (ii) every other person who is a party to the proceedings.

(4) If the person referred to in paragraph (2) wishes to act as a litigation friend for the protected party, he must file and serve a copy of the court order which appointed him on those persons mentioned in paragraph (3)(b).

143 Litigation friend by court order

(1) The court may make an order appointing –

(a) the Official Solicitor; or
(b) some other person,

to act as a litigation friend.

(2) The court may act under paragraph (1) –

(a) either on its own initiative or on the application of any person; but
(b) only with the consent of the person to be appointed.

(3) An application for an order under paragraph (1) must be supported by evidence.

(4) The court may not appoint a litigation friend under this rule unless it is satisfied that the person to be appointed satisfies the conditions specified in rule 140(1).

(5) The court may at any stage of the proceedings give directions as to the appointment of a litigation friend.

144 Court's power to prevent a person from acting as litigation friend or to order change

(1) The court may either on its own initiative or on the application of any person –

(a) direct that a person may not act as a litigation friend;
(b) terminate a litigation friend's appointment; or
(c) appoint a new litigation friend in place of an existing one.

(2) An application for an order under paragraph (1) must be supported by evidence.

(3) The court may not appoint a litigation friend under this rule unless it is satisfied that the person to be appointed satisfies the conditions specified in rule 140(1).

145 Appointment of litigation friend by court order – supplementary

The applicant must serve a copy of an application for an order under rule 143 or 144 on –

(a) the person on whom an application form is to be served in accordance with rule 32 (service on children and protected parties);
(b) every other person who is a party to the proceedings;
(c) any person who is the litigation friend, or who is purporting to act as the litigation friend, when the application is made; and

(d) unless he is the applicant, the person who it is proposed should be the litigation friend,

as soon as practicable and in any event within 21 days of the date on which it was issued.

146 Procedure where appointment of litigation friend comes to an end – for a child or protected party

(1) This rule applies –

(a) when a child reaches 18, provided he is neither –
(i) P; nor
(ii) a protected party; and
(b) where a protected party ceases to be a person who lacks capacity to conduct the proceedings himself.

(2) Where paragraph (1)(a) applies, the litigation friend's appointment ends.

(3) Where paragraph (1)(b) applies, the litigation friend's appointment continues until it is brought to an end by a court order

(4) An application for an order under paragraph (3) may be made by –

(a) the former protected party;
(b) his litigation friend; or
(c) any other person who is a party to the proceedings.

(5) The applicant must serve a copy of the application notice seeking an order under this rule on all parties to the proceedings as soon as practicable and in any event within 21 days of the date on which it was issued.

(6) Where paragraph (2) applies the child must serve notice on every other party –

(a) stating that he has reached full age;
(b) stating that the appointment of the litigation friend has ended; and
(c) providing his address for service.

(7) Where paragraph (3) applies, the former protected party must provide his address for service to all other parties to the proceedings.

147 Procedure where appointment of litigation friend comes to an end – for P

(1) This rule applies where P ceases to be a person who lacks capacity to conduct the proceedings himself but continues to lack capacity in relation to the matter or matters to which the application relates.

(2) The litigation friend's appointment continues until it is brought to an end by a court order.

(3) An application for an order under paragraph (2) may be made by –

(a) P;
(b) his litigation friend; or
(c) any other person who is a party to the proceedings.

(4) The applicant must serve a copy of the application notice seeking an order under this rule on all other parties to the proceedings as soon as practicable and in any event within 21 days of the date on which it was issued.

(5) Where the court makes an order under this rule, P must provide his address for service to all other parties to the proceedings.

148 Procedure where P ceases to lack capacity

(1) This rule applies where P ceases to lack capacity both to conduct the proceedings himself and in relation to the matter or matters to which the application relates.

(2) The litigation friend's appointment continues until it is brought to an end by a court order.

(3) An application may be made by –

- *(a) P;*
- *(b) his litigation friend; or*
- *(c) any other person who is a party to the proceedings,*

for the proceedings to come to an end.

(4) The applicant must serve a copy of the application notice seeking an order under this rule on all parties to the proceedings as soon as practicable and in any event within 21 days of the date on which it was issued.

149 Practice direction in relation to litigation friends

A practice direction may make additional or different provision in relation to litigation friends.

[PART 17]
[LITIGATION FRIENDS AND RULE 3A REPRESENTATIVES]

Amendments—Part substituted with effect from 1 July 2015 by virtue of SI 2015/548.

[Section 1]

[Litigation friends]

Amendments—Section title inserted with effect from 1 July 2015 by virtue of SI 2015/548.

[140 Who may act as a litigation friend]

[(1) A person may act as a litigation friend on behalf of a person mentioned in paragraph (2) if that person –

- (a) can fairly and competently conduct proceedings on behalf of that person; and
- (b) has no interests adverse to those of that person.

(2) The persons for whom a litigation friend may act are –

- (a) P;
- (b) a child;
- (c) a protected party.]

Amendments—Provision substituted with effect from 1 July 2015 by virtue of SI 2015/548.

[141 Requirement for a litigation friend]

[(1) This rule does not apply to P (whether P is an adult or a child).

(2) A protected party (if a party to the proceedings) must have a litigation friend.

(3) A child (if a party to the proceedings) must have a litigation friend to conduct those proceedings on that child's behalf unless the court makes an order under paragraph (4).

(4) The court may make an order permitting a child to conduct proceedings without a litigation friend.

(5) An application for an order under paragraph (4) –

- (a) may be made by the child;
- (b) if the child already has a litigation friend, must be made on notice to the litigation friend; and
- (c) if the child has no litigation friend, may be made without notice.

(6) Where –

- (a) the court has made an order under paragraph (4); and
- (b) it subsequently appears to the court that it is desirable for a litigation friend to conduct the proceedings on behalf of the child,

the court may appoint a person to the child's litigation friend.]

Amendments—Provision substituted with effect from 1 July 2015 by virtue of SI 2015/548.

[142 Litigation friend without a court order]

[(1) This rule does not apply –

- (a) in relation to P;
- (b) where the court has appointed a person under rule 143 or 144; or .
- (c) where the Official Solicitor is to act as a litigation friend.

(2) A deputy with the power to conduct legal proceedings in the name of a protected party or on the protected party's behalf is entitled to be a litigation friend of the protected party in any proceedings to which the deputy's power relates.

(3) If no-one has been appointed by the court or, in the case of a protected party, there is no deputy with the power to conduct proceedings, a person who wishes to act as a litigation friend must –

- (a) file a certificate of suitability stating that they satisfy the conditions in rule 140(1); and
- (b) serve the certificate of suitability on –
  - (i) the person on whom an application form is to be served in accordance with rule 32 (service on children and protected parties); and
  - (ii) every other person who is a party to the proceedings.

(4) If the person referred to in paragraph (2) wishes to act as a litigation friend for the protected party, that person must file and serve on the persons mentioned in paragraph (3)(b) a copy of the court order which appointed that person.]

Amendments—Provision substituted with effect from 1 July 2015 by virtue of SI 2015/548.

[143 Litigation friend by court order]

[(1) The court may make an order appointing –

(a) the Official Solicitor; or
(b) some other person,

to act as a litigation friend for a protected party, a child or P.

(2) The court may make an order under paragraph (1) –

(a) either on its own initiative or on the application of any person; but
(b) only with the consent of the person to be appointed.

(3) An application for an order under paragraph (1) must be supported by evidence.

(4) The court may not appoint a litigation friend under this rule unless it is satisfied that the person to be appointed satisfies the conditions in rule 140(1).

(5) The court may at any stage of the proceedings give directions as to the appointment of a litigation friend.

(Rule 3A requires the court to consider how P should participate in the proceedings, which may be by way of being made a party and the appointment of a litigation friend under this Part.)]

Amendments—Provision substituted with effect from 1 July 2015 by virtue of SI 2015/548.

[144 Court's power to prevent a person from acting as a litigation friend or to bring an end to an appointment of a person as a litigation friend or to appoint another one]

[(1) The court may either on its own initiative or on the application of any person –

(a) direct that a person may not act as a litigation friend;
(b) bring to an end a litigation friend's appointment; or
(c) appoint a new litigation friend in place of an existing one.

(2) If an application for an order under paragraph (1) is based on the conduct of the litigation friend, it must be supported by evidence.

(3) The court may not appoint a litigation friend under this rule unless it is satisfied that the person to be appointed satisfies the conditions in rule 140(1).

(4) The appointment of a litigation friend continues until brought to an end by court order.

(Rule 87 applies if P has capacity in relation to the matter or matters to which the application relates.)]

Amendments—Provision substituted with effect from 1 July 2015 by virtue of SI 2015/548.

[145 Appointment of litigation friend by court order – supplementary]

[The applicant must serve a copy of an application for an order under rule 143 or 144 on –

(a) the person on whom an application form is to be served in accordance with rule 32 (service on children and protected parties);
(b) every other person who is a party to the proceedings;
(c) any person who is the litigation friend, or who is purporting to act as the litigation friend, when the application is made; and

(d) unless that person is the applicant, the person who it is proposed should be the litigation friend,

as soon as practicable and in any event within 14 days of the date on which the application was issued.]

Amendments—Provision substituted with effect from 1 July 2015 by virtue of SI 2015/548.

[145A Procedure where appointment of a litigation friend comes to an end for a child]

[When a child reaches 18, provided the child is neither –

(a) P; nor
(b) a protected party,

the litigation friend's appointment ends and the child must serve notice on every other party –

(i) stating that the child has reached full age;
(ii) stating that the appointment of the litigation friend has ended; and
(iii) providing an address for service.]

Amendments—Provision inserted with effect from 1 July 2015 by virtue of SI 2015/548.

[146 Practice direction in relation to litigation friends]

[A practice direction may make additional or supplementary provision in relation to litigation friends.]

Amendments—Provision substituted with effect from 1 July 2015 by virtue of SI 2015/548.

[Section 2]

[Rule 3A representatives]

Amendments—Section title inserted with effect from 1 July 2015 by virtue of SI 2015/548.

[146A Interpretation]

[In this Section, references to 'rule 3A representatives' are references to both accredited legal representatives and representatives.

('Accredited legal representative' and "'representative' are defined in rule 6.)]

Amendments—Provision inserted with effect from 1 July 2015 by virtue of SI 2015/548.

[147 Who may act as a rule 3A representative for P]

[A person may act as an accredited legal representative, or a representative, for P, if that person can fairly and competently discharge his or her functions on behalf of P.]

Amendments—Provision substituted with effect from 1 July 2015 by virtue of SI 2015/548.

[148 Rule 3A representative by court order]

[(1) The court may make an order appointing a person to act as a representative, or an accredited legal representative, for P.

(2) The court may make an order under paragraph (1) –

(a) either of its own initiative or on the application of any person; but
(b) only with the consent of the person to be appointed.

(3) The court may not appoint a representative or an accredited legal representative under this rule unless it is satisfied that the person to be appointed satisfies the conditions in rule 147.

(4) The court may at any stage of the proceedings give directions as to the terms of appointment of a representative or an accredited legal representative.

(Rule 3A requires the court to consider how P should participate in the proceedings, which may be by way of the appointment of a representative or accredited legal representative under this Part.)]

Amendments—Provision substituted with effect from 1 July 2015 by virtue of SI 2015/548.

[148A Application by rule 3A representative or by P for directions]

[A representative, an accredited legal representative or P may, at any time and without giving notice to the other parties, apply to the court for directions relating to the performance, terms of appointment or continuation of the appointment of the representative or accredited legal representative.]

Amendments—Provision inserted with effect from 1 July 2015 by virtue of SI 2015/548.

[148B Court's power to prevent a person from acting as a rule 3A representative or to bring an end to an appointment of a person as a rule 3A representative or appoint another one]

[(1) The court may, either of its own initiative or on the application of any person –

(a) direct that a person may not act as a representative or accredited legal representative;
(b) bring to an end a representative's or accredited legal representative's appointment;
(c) appoint a new representative or accredited legal representative in place of an existing one; or
(d) vary the terms of a representative's or accredited legal representative's appointment.

(2) If an application for an order under paragraph (1) is based on the conduct of the representative or accredited legal representative, it must be supported by evidence.

(3) The court may not appoint a representative or accredited legal representative under this rule unless it is satisfied that the person to be appointed satisfies the conditions in rule 147.

(4) The appointment of a representative or accredited legal representative continues until brought to an end by court order.

(5) The court must bring to an end the appointment of a representative or an accredited legal representative if P has capacity to appoint such a representative and does not wish the appointment by the court to continue.]

Amendments—Provision inserted with effect from 1 July 2015 by virtue of SI 2015/548.

[148C Appointment of rule 3A representative by court order – supplementary]

[The applicant must serve a copy of an application for an order under rule 148 or rule 148B on –

(a) the person on whom an application form is to be served in accordance with rule 32 (service on children and protected parties);
(b) every other person who is a party to the proceedings;
(c) any person who is the representative, or accredited legal representative, purporting to act as such representative, when the application is made; and
(d) unless that person is the applicant, the person who it is proposed should be the representative or accredited legal representative,

as soon as practicable and in any event within 14 days of the date on which the application was issued.]

Amendments—Provision inserted with effect from 1 July 2015 by virtue of SI 2015/548.

[149 Practice direction in relation to rule 3A representatives]

[A practice direction may make additional or supplementary provision in relation to representatives or accredited legal representatives.]

Amendments—Provision substituted with effect from 1 July 2015 by virtue of SI 2015/548.

PART 18
CHANGE OF SOLICITOR

150 Change of solicitor

(1) This rule applies where a party to proceedings –

(a) for whom a solicitor is acting wants to change his solicitor or act in person; or
(b) after having conducted the proceedings in person, appoints a solicitor to act on his behalf (except where the solicitor is appointed only to act as an advocate for a hearing).

(2) The party proposing the change must –

(a) file a notice of the change with the court; and
(b) serve the notice of the change on every other party to the proceedings and, if there is one, on the solicitor who will cease to act.

(3) The notice must state the party's address for service.

(4) The notice filed at court must state that it has been served as required by paragraph (2)(b).

(5) Where there is a solicitor who will cease to act, he will continue to be considered the party's solicitor unless and until –

- (a) the notice is filed and served in accordance with paragraphs (2), (3) and (4); or
- (b) the court makes an order under rule 152 and the order is served in accordance with that rule.

151 Legally aided persons

(1) Where the certificate of any person ('A') who is a legally aided person is revoked or withdrawn –

- (a) the solicitor who acted for A will cease to be the solicitor acting in the case as soon as his retainer is determined under regulation 24 or 41 of the Civil Legal Aid (Procedure) Regulations 2012; and
- (b) if A wishes to continue and appoints a solicitor to act on his behalf, rule 150(2), (3) and (4) will apply as if A had previously conducted the application in person.

(2) In this rule, 'certificate' means a certificate issued under the Civil Legal Aid (Procedure) Regulations 2012.

152 Order that a solicitor has ceased to act

(1) A solicitor may apply for an order declaring that he has ceased to be the solicitor acting for a party.

(2) Where an application is made under this rule –

- (a) the solicitor must serve the application notice on the party for whom the solicitor is acting, unless the court directs otherwise; and
- (b) the application must be supported by evidence.

(3) Where the court makes an order that a solicitor has ceased to act, the solicitor must –

- (a) serve a copy of the order on every other party to the proceedings; and
- (b) file a certificate of service.

153 Removal of solicitor who has ceased to act on application of another party

(1) Where –

- (a) a solicitor who has acted for a party –
  - (i) has died;
  - (ii) has become bankrupt;
  - (iii) has ceased to practice; or
  - (iv) cannot be found; and
- (b) the party has not served a notice of a change of solicitor or notice of intention to act in person as required by rule 150,

any other party may apply for an order declaring that the solicitor has ceased to be the solicitor acting for the other party in the case.

(2) Where an application is made under this rule, the applicant must serve the application on the party to whose solicitor the application relates, unless the court directs otherwise.

(3) Where the court makes an order under this rule –

- (a) the court will give directions about serving a copy of the order on every other party to the proceedings; and
- (b) where the order is served by a party, that party must file a certificate of service.

154 Practice direction relating to change of solicitor

A practice direction may make additional or different provision in relation to change of solicitor.

PART 19
COSTS

155 Interpretation

(1) In this Part –

- *(a) 'additional liability' means the percentage increase, the insurance premium, or the additional amount in respect of provision made by a membership organisation, as the case may be;*
- *(b) 'authorised court officer' means any officer of the Supreme Court Costs Office, whom the Lord Chancellor has authorised to assess costs;*
- *(c) 'costs' include fees, charges, disbursements, expenses, reimbursement permitted to a litigant in person, any additional liability incurred under a funding arrangement and any fee or reward charged by a lay representative for acting on behalf of a party in proceedings;*
- *(d) 'costs judge' means a taxing Master of the Supreme Court;*
- *(e) 'costs officer' means a costs judge or an authorised court officer;*
- *(f) 'detailed assessment' means the procedure by which the amount of costs or remuneration is decided by a costs officer in accordance with Part 47 of the Civil Procedure Rules 1998 (which are applied to proceedings under these Rules, with modifications, by rule 160);*
- *(g) 'fixed costs' are to be construed in accordance with the relevant practice direction;*
- *(h) 'fund' includes any estate or property held for the benefit of any person or class of persons and any fund to which a trustee or personal representative is entitled in his capacity as such;*
- *(i) 'funding arrangement' means an arrangement where a person has –*
  - *(i) entered into a conditional fee agreement or a collective conditional fee agreement which provides for a success fee within the meaning of section 58(2) of the Courts and Legal Services Act 1990;*
  - *(ii) taken out an insurance policy to which section 29 of the Access to Justice Act 1999 (recovery of insurance premiums by way of costs) applies; or*
  - *(iii) made an agreement with a membership organisation to meet his legal costs;*
- *(j) 'insurance premium' means a sum of money paid or payable for insurance*

against the risk of incurring a costs liability in the proceedings, taken out after the event that is the subject matter of the claim;

- *(k)* *'membership organisation' means a body prescribed for the purposes of section 30 of the Access to Justice Act 1999 (recovery where body undertakes to meet costs liabilities);*
- *(l)* *'paying party' means a party liable to pay costs;*
- *(m)* *'percentage increase' means the percentage by which the amount of a legal representative's fee can be increased in accordance with a conditional fee agreement which provides for a success fee;*
- *(n)* *'receiving party' means a party entitled to be paid costs;*
- *(o)* *'summary assessment' means the procedure by which the court, when making an order about costs, orders payment of a sum of money instead of fixed costs or 'detailed assessment'.*

[(1) In this Part –

"authorised court officer" means any officer of the Senior Courts Costs Office whom the Lord Chancellor has authorised to assess costs;

"costs" include fees, charges, disbursements, expenses, remuneration and any reimbursement allowed to a litigant in person;

"costs judge" means a taxing Master of the Senior Courts;

"costs officer" means a costs judge or an authorised court officer;

"detailed assessment" means the procedure by which the amount of costs or remuneration is decided by a costs officer in accordance with Part 47 of the Civil Procedure Rules 1998 (which are applied to proceedings under these Rules, with modifications, by rule 160);

"fixed costs" are to be construed in accordance with the relevant practice direction;

"fund" includes any estate or property held for the benefit of any person or class of persons, and any fund to which a trustee or personal representative is entitled in that capacity;

"paying party" means a party liable to pay costs;

"pro bono representation" means representation provided free of charge;

"receiving party" means a party entitled to be paid costs;

"summary assessment" means the procedure by which the court, when making an order about costs, orders payment of a sum of money instead of fixed costs or detailed assessment.]

(2) The costs to which the rules in this Part apply include –

- (a) where the costs may be assessed by the court, costs payable by a client to *his solicitor*[their legal representative]; and
- (b) costs which are payable by one party to another party under the terms of a contract, where the court makes an order for an assessment of those costs.

(3) Where advocacy or litigation services are provided to a client under a conditional fee agreement, costs are recoverable under this Part notwithstanding that the client is liable to pay his legal representative's fees and expenses only to the extent that sums are recovered in respect of the proceedings, whether by way of costs or otherwise.

(4) In paragraph (3), the reference to a conditional fee agreement *is to an agreement which satisfies all the conditions applicable to it by virtue of*[means an agreement enforceable under] section 58 of the Courts and Legal Services Act 1990.

Amendments—Words in italics revoked and words in square brackets inserted with effect from 1 July 2015 by virtue of SI 2015/548.

156 Property and affairs – the general rule

Where the proceedings concern P's property and affairs the general rule is that the costs of the proceedings or of that part of the proceedings that concerns P's property and affairs, shall be paid by P or charged to his estate.

157 Personal welfare – the general rule

Where the proceedings concern P's personal welfare the general rule is that there will be no order as to the costs of the proceedings or of that part of the proceedings that concerns P's personal welfare.

158 Apportioning costs – the general rule

Where the proceedings concern both property and affairs and personal welfare the court, insofar as practicable, will apportion the costs as between the respective issues.

159 Departing from the general rule

(1) The court may depart from rules 156 to 158 if the circumstances so justify, and in deciding whether departure is justified the court will have regard to all the circumstances, including –

- (a) the conduct of the parties;
- (b) whether a party has succeeded on part of his case, even if he has not been wholly successful; and
- (c) the role of any public body involved in the proceedings.

(2) The conduct of the parties includes –

- (a) conduct before, as well as during, the proceedings;
- (b) whether it was reasonable for a party to raise, pursue or contest a particular issue;
- (c) the manner in which a party has made or responded to an application or a particular issue; *and*
- (d) whether a party who has succeeded in his application or response to an application, in whole or in part, exaggerated any matter contained in his application or response.[; and
- (e) any failure by a party to comply with a rule, practice direction or court order.]

(3) Without prejudice to rules 156 to 158 and the foregoing provisions of this rule, the court may permit a party to recover their fixed costs in accordance with the relevant practice direction.

Amendments—Word in italics revoked and words in square brackets inserted with effect from 1 July 2015 by virtue of SI 2015/548.

160 Rules about costs in the Civil Procedure Rules to apply

(1) Subject to the provisions of these Rules, Parts 44, 47 and 48 of the Civil Procedure Rules 1998 ('the 1998 Rules') shall apply with the modifications in this

rule and such other modifications as may be appropriate, to costs incurred in relation to proceedings under these Rules as they apply to costs incurred in relation to proceedings in the High Court.

(2) The provisions of Part 47 of the 1998 Rules shall apply with the modifications in this rule and such other modifications as may be appropriate, to a detailed assessment of the remuneration of a deputy under these Rules as they apply to a detailed assessment of costs in proceedings to which the 1998 Rules apply.

(3) Where the definitions in Part 43 (referred to in Parts 44, 47 and 48) of the 1998 Rules are different from the definitions in rule 155 of these Rules, the latter shall prevail.

(4) Rules 44.1, 44.3(1) to (5), 44.6, 44.7, 44.9, 44.10, 44.11. 44.12 and 44.12A of the 1998 Rules do not apply.

(5) In rule 44.17 of the 1998 Rules, the references to Parts 45 and 46 do not apply.

(6) In rule 47.3(1)(c) of the 1998 Rules, the words 'unless the costs are being assessed under rule 48.5 (costs where money is payable to a child or a patient)' are removed.

(7) In rule 47.3(2) of the 1998 Rules, the words 'or a district judge' are removed.

(8) Rule 47.4(3) and (4) of the 1998 Rules do not apply.

(9) Rules 47.9(4), 47.10 and 47.11 of the 1998 Rules do not apply where the costs are to be paid by P or charged to his estate.

(10) Rules 48.2, 48.3, 48.6A, and 48.10 of the 1998 Rules do not apply.

(11) Rule 48.1(1) of the 1998 Rules is removed and is replaced by the following: 'This paragraph applies where a person applies for an order for specific disclosure before the commencement of proceedings'.

[160 Rules about costs in the Civil Procedure Rules to apply]

[(1) Subject to the provisions of these Rules, Parts 44, 46 and 47 of the Civil Procedure Rules 1998 ('the 1998 Rules') apply with the modifications in this rule and such other modifications as may be appropriate, to costs incurred in relation to proceedings under these Rules as they apply to costs incurred in relation to proceedings in the High Court.

(2) Rules 3.12 to 3.18 of the 1998 Rules and Practice Direction 3E supporting those Rules do not apply in relation to proceedings under these Rules.

(3) The provisions of Part 47 of the 1998 Rules apply with the modifications in this rule and such other modifications as may be appropriate, to a detailed assessment of the remuneration of a deputy under these Rules as they apply to a detailed assessment of costs in proceedings to which the 1998 Rules apply.

(4) Where the definitions in Part 44 (referred to in Parts 44, 46 and 47) of the 1998 Rules are different from the definitions in rule 155 of these Rules, the latter definitions prevail.

(5) Rules 44.2(1) to (5), 44.5, 44.6, 44.9 and 44.13 to 44.18 of the 1998 Rules do not apply.

(6) For rule 46.1(1) of the 1998 Rules there is substituted –

> '(1) This paragraph applies where a person applies for an order for specific disclosure before the commencement of proceedings.'.

(7) Rules 46.2, 46.5 and 46.10 to 46.14 of the 1998 Rules do not apply.

(8) In rule 47.3(1)(c) of the 1998 Rules, the words 'unless the costs are being assessed under rule 46.4 (costs where money is payable to a child or protected party)' are omitted.

(9) In rule 47.3(2) of the 1998 Rules, the words "or a District Judge" are omitted.

(10) Rule 47.4(3) and (4) of the 1998 Rules do not apply.

(11) Rules 47.9(4), 47.10 and 47.11 of the 1998 Rules do not apply where the costs are to be paid by P or charged to P's estate.]

Amendments—Provision substituted with effect from 1 July 2015 by virtue of SI 2015/548.

161 Detailed assessment of costs

(1) Where the court orders costs to be assessed by way of detailed assessment, the detailed assessment proceedings shall take place in the High Court.

(2) A fee is payable in respect of the detailed assessment of costs and on an appeal against a decision made in a detailed assessment of costs.

(3) Where a detailed assessment of costs has taken place, the amount payable by P is the amount which the court certifies as payable.

162 Employment of a solicitor by two or more persons

Where two or more persons having the same interest in relation to a matter act in relation to the proceedings by separate legal representatives, they shall not be permitted more than one set of costs of the representation unless and to the extent that the court certifies that the circumstances justify separate representation

163 Costs of the Official Solicitor

Any costs incurred by the Official Solicitor in relation to proceedings under these Rules or in carrying out any directions given by the court and not provided for by remuneration under rule 167 shall be paid by such persons or out of such funds as the court may direct.

164 Procedure for assessing costs

Where the court orders a party, or P, to pay costs to another party it may either –

(a) make a summary assessment of the costs; or
(b) order a detailed assessment of the costs by a costs officer,

unless any rule, practice direction or other enactment provides otherwise.

165 Costs following P's death

An order or direction that costs incurred during P's lifetime be paid out of or charged on his estate may be made within 6 years after P's death.

166 Costs orders in favour of or against non-parties

(1) Where the court is considering whether to make a costs order in favour of or against a person who is not a party to proceedings[, that person must be] –

- (a) *that person must be* added as a party to the proceedings for the purposes of costs only; *and*
- [(aa) served with such documents as the court may direct; and]
- (b) *he must be* given a reasonable opportunity to attend *a hearing*[any hearing] at which the court will consider the matter further.

(2) This rule does not apply where the court is considering whether to make an order against the *Legal Services Commission*[Lord Chancellor in proceedings in which the Lord Chancellor has provided legal aid to a party to the proceedings].

Amendments—Words in italics revoked and words in square brackets inserted with effect from 1 July 2015 by virtue of SI 2015/548.

167 Remuneration of a deputy, donee or attorney

(1) Where the court orders that a deputy, donee or attorney is entitled to remuneration out of P's estate for discharging his functions as such, the court may make such order as it thinks fit, including an order that –

- (a) he be paid a fixed amount;
- (b) he be paid at a specified rate; or
- (c) the amount of the remuneration shall be determined in accordance with the schedule of fees set out in the relevant practice direction.

(2) Any amount permitted by the court under paragraph (1) shall constitute a debt due from P's estate.

(3) The court may order a detailed assessment of the remuneration by a costs officer, in accordance with rule 164(b).

168 Practice Direction as to costs

A practice direction may make further provision in respect of costs in proceedings.

PART 20
APPEALS

169 Scope of this Part

This Part applies to an appeal against any decision of the court except where, in relation to those cases that are to be dealt with in accordance with Part 22 (transitory and transitional provisions), Part 22 makes different provision.

[169 Scope of this Part]

[This Part applies to an appeal against any decision of the court.]

Amendments—Provision substituted with effect from 6 April 2015 by virtue of SI 2015/548.

170 Interpretation

(1) In the following provisions of this Part –

(a) 'appeal judge' means a judge of the court to whom an appeal is made;
(b) 'first instance judge' means the judge of the court from whose decision an appeal is brought;
(c) 'appellant' means the person who brings or seeks to bring an appeal;
(d) 'respondent' means –
  (i) a person other than the appellant who was a party to the proceedings before the first instance judge and who is affected by the appeal; or
  (ii) a person who is permitted or directed by the first instance judge or the appeal judge to be a party to the appeal.[; and
(e) 'a second appeal' means an appeal from a decision of a judge of the court which was itself made on appeal from a judge of the court.]

(2) In this Part, where the expression 'permission' is used it means 'permission to appeal' unless otherwise stated.

Amendments—Full stop at the end of sub-paragraph 1(d) revoked and words in square brackets inserted with effect from 6 April 2015 by virtue of SI 2015/548 (subject to transitional provisions).

171 Dealing with appeals

(1) The court may deal with an appeal or any part of an appeal at a hearing or without a hearing.

(2) In considering whether it is necessary to hold a hearing, the court shall have regard to the matters set out in rule 84(3).

[(3) Any person bound by an order of the court by virtue of rule 74 (persons to be bound as if parties) may seek permission under this Part.

(4) All parties to an appeal must comply with any relevant practice direction.

(5) Where permission is required, it is to be granted or refused in accordance with this Part.]

(Rule 89 provides for reconsideration of orders made without a hearing or without notice to a person.)

Amendments—Words in square brackets inserted with effect from 1 July 2015 by virtue of SI 2015/548.

[171A Destination of appeals]

[(1) An appeal from a decision of a judge of the court shall lie to the Court of Appeal in the following cases –

(a) where it is an appeal from a decision of a Tier 3 Judge; or
(b) where it is a second appeal.

(2) Subject to paragraph (1) and to any alternative provision made by the relevant practice direction –

(a) where the first instance judge was a Tier 1 Judge, any appeal shall be heard by a Tier 2 Judge;
(b) where the first instance judge was a Tier 2 Judge, any appeal shall be heard by a Tier 3 Judge.

(3) No appeal may be made against a decision of a court officer authorised under rule 7A.

(A decision of a court officer authorised under rule 7A can be reconsidered by a judge under rule 89.)]

Amendments—Provision inserted with effect from 6 April 2015 by virtue of SI 2015/548 (subject to transitional provisions).

[171B Permission to appeal – appeals to the Court of Appeal]

[(1) Subject to rule 172A, an appeal to the Court of Appeal against a decision of a judge of the court may not be made without permission.

(2) Where an appeal to the Court of Appeal is made from a decision of a Tier 3 Judge, permission may be granted by the first instance judge or by the Court of Appeal, unless the appeal is a second appeal.

(3) Where an appeal to the Court of Appeal is a second appeal, permission may only be granted by the Court of Appeal.

(4) No appeal shall lie against –

(a) the granting or refusal of permission under this rule; or
(b) an order allowing an extension of time for appealing from an order.

(The procedure for an appeal from a decision of a judge of the court to the Court of Appeal, including requirements for permission, is governed by the Civil Procedure Rules 1998.)]

Amendments—Provision inserted with effect from 6 April 2015 by virtue of SI 2015/548 (subject to transitional provisions).

172 Permission to appeal

(1) Subject to paragraph (8), an appeal against a decision of the court may not be made without permission.

(2) Any person bound by an order of the court by virtue of rule 74 (persons to be bound as if parties) may seek permission to appeal under this Part.

(3) Permission is to be granted or refused in accordance with this Part.

(4) An application for permission to appeal may be made to the first instance judge or the appeal judge.

(5) Where an application for permission is refused by the first instance judge, a further application for permission may be made in accordance with paragraphs (6) and (7).

(6) Where the decision sought to be appealed is a decision of a district judge, permission may be granted or refused by –

(a) the President;
(b) the Vice-President;
(c) one of the other judges nominated by virtue of section 46(2)(a) to (c) of the Act; or
(d) a circuit judge.

(7) Where the decision sought to be appealed is a decision of a circuit judge, permission may only be granted or refused by one of the judges mentioned in paragraph (6)(a) to (c).

(8) Permission is not required to appeal against an order for committal to prison.

[172 Permission to appeal – other cases]

[(1) Subject to rules 171B and 172A, an appeal against a decision of the court may not be made without permission.

(2) An application for permission to appeal may be made to –

(a) the first instance judge; or .
(b) another judge who satisfies the relevant condition in paragraph (4) or (5).

(3) Where an application for permission is refused by the first instance judge, a further application for permission may be made to a judge who satisfies the relevant condition in paragraph (4) or (5).

(4) Where the decision sought to be appealed is a decision of a Tier 1 Judge, permission may also be granted or refused by –

(a) a Tier 2 Judge; or
(b) a Tier 3 Judge.

(5) Where the decision sought to be appealed is a decision of a Tier 2 Judge, permission may also be granted or refused by a Tier 3 Judge.

(6) Subject to paragraph (7) and except where another rule or a practice direction provides otherwise, where a judge who satisfies the relevant condition in paragraph (4) or (5), without a hearing, refuses permission to appeal against the decision of the first instance judge, the person seeking permission may request the decision to be reconsidered at a hearing.

(7) Where a Tier 3 Judge or the Senior Judge refuses permission to appeal without a hearing and considers that the application is totally without merit, that judge may order that the person seeking permission may not request the decision to be reconsidered at a hearing.

(8) Subject to paragraph (6), no appeal shall lie against –

(a) the granting or refusal of permission under this rule; or
(b) an order allowing an extension of time for appealing from an order.]

Amendments—Provision substituted with effect from 6 April 2015 by virtue of SI 2015/548 (subject to transitional provisions).

[172A Appeal against an order for committal to prison]

[Permission is not required to appeal against an order for committal to prison.]

Amendments—Provision inserted with effect from 6 April 2015 by virtue of SI 2015/548 (subject to transitional provisions).

173 Matters to be taken into account when considering an application for permission

(1) Permission to appeal shall be granted only where –

(a) the court considers that the appeal would have a real prospect of success; or
(b) there is some other compelling reason why the appeal should be heard.

(2) An order giving permission may –

(a) limit the issues to be heard; and
(b) be made subject to conditions.

[(3) Paragraphs (1) and (2) do not apply to second appeals.]

Amendments—Words in square brackets inserted with effect from 6 April 2015 by virtue of SI 2015/548 (subject to transitional provisions).

174 Parties to comply with the practice direction

All parties to an appeal must comply with any relevant practice direction.

[174 Power to treat application for permission to appeal as application for reconsideration under rule 89]

[(1) Where a person seeking permission to appeal a decision would be entitled to seek reconsideration of that decision under rule 89 (or would have been so entitled had the application been made within 21 days of the date of that decision) –

(a) a practice direction may provide; or
(b) the court may direct,

that an application for permission shall be treated as an application for reconsideration under rule 89.

(2) In any case where paragraph (1) applies, the decision in question shall be reconsidered in accordance with the provisions of rule 89.]

Amendments—Provision substituted with effect from 6 April 2015 by virtue of SI 2015/548 (subject to transitional provisions).

175 Appellant's notice

(1) Where the appellant seeks permission *from the appeal judge*[a judge other than the first instance judge], it must be requested in the appellant's notice.

(2) The appellant must file an appellant's notice at the court within –

(a) such period as may be directed or specified in the order of the first instance judge; or
(b) where that judge makes no such direction or order, 21 days after the date of the decision being appealed.

(3) The court will issue the appellant's notice and unless it orders otherwise, the appellant must serve the appellant's notice on each respondent and on such other persons as the court may direct, as soon as practicable and in any event within 21 days of the date on which it was issued.

(4) The appellant must file a certificate of service within 7 days beginning with the date on which he served the appellant's notice.

Amendments—Words in italics revoked and words in square brackets inserted with effect from 6 April 2015 by virtue of SI 2015/548 (subject to transitional provisions). Note that the word 'from' has been revoked in error.

176 Respondent's notice

(1) A respondent who –

(a) is seeking permission from *the appeal judge to appeal*[a judge other than the first instance judge]; or
(b) wishes to ask the appeal judge to uphold the order of the first instance judge for reasons different from or additional to those given by the first instance judge,

must file a respondent's notice.

(2) Where the respondent seeks permission from *the appeal judge*[a judge other than the first instance judge], permission must be requested in the respondent's notice.

(3) A respondent's notice must be filed within –

(a) such period as may be directed by the first instance judge; or
(b) where the first instance judge makes no such direction, 21 days beginning with the date referred to in paragraph (4).

(4) The date is the soonest of –

(a) the date on which the respondent is served with the appellant's notice where –
 (i) permission *to appeal* was given by the first instance judge; or
 (ii) permission *to appeal* is not required;
(b) the date on which the respondent is served with notification that *the appeal judge*[a judge other than the first instance judge] has given the appellant permission *to appeal*; or
(c) the date on which the respondent is served with the notification that the application for permission *to appeal* and the appeal itself are to be heard together.

(5) The court will issue a respondent's notice and, unless it orders otherwise, the respondent must serve the respondent's notice on the appellant, any other respondent and on such other parties as the court may direct, as soon as practicable and in any event within 21 days of the date on which it was issued.

(6) The respondent must file a certificate of service within 7 days beginning with the date on which the copy of the respondent's notice was served.

Amendments—Words in italics revoked and words in square brackets inserted with effect from 6 April 2015 by virtue of SI 2015/548 (subject to transitional provisions).

177 Variation of time

(1) An application to vary the time limit for filing an appellant's or respondent's notice must be made to the appeal judge.

(2) The parties may not agree to extend any date or time limit for or in respect of an appeal set by –

(a) these Rules;
(b) the relevant practice direction; or
(c) an order of the appeal judge or the first instance judge.

Amendments—Words in italics revoked with effect from 6 April 2015 by virtue of SI 2015/548 (subject to transitional provisions).

178 Power of appeal judge on appeal

(1) In relation to an appeal, an appeal judge has all the powers of the first instance judge whose decision is being appealed.

(2) In particular, the appeal judge has the power to –

(a) affirm, set aside or vary any order made by the first instance judge;
(b) refer any claim or issue to that judge for determination;
(c) order a new hearing;
(d) make a costs order.

(3) The appeal judge may exercise his powers in relation to the whole or part of an order made by the first instance judge.

179 Determination of appeals

(1) An appeal will be limited to a review of the decision of the first instance judge unless –

(a) a practice direction makes different provision for a particular category of appeal; or
(b) the appeal judge considers that in the circumstances of the appeal it would be in the interests of justice to hold a re-hearing.

(2) Unless he orders otherwise, the appeal judge will not receive –

(a) oral evidence; or
(b) evidence that was not before the first instance judge.

(3) The appeal judge will allow an appeal where the decision of the first instance judge was –

(a) wrong; or
(b) unjust, because of a serious procedural or other irregularity in the proceedings before the first instance judge.

(4) The appeal judge may draw any inference of fact that he considers justified on the evidence.

(5) At the hearing of the appeal a party may not rely upon a matter not contained in his appellant's or respondent's notice unless the appeal judge gives permission.

180 Allocation

Except in accordance with the relevant practice direction –

(a) an appeal from a first instance decision of a circuit judge shall be heard by a judge of the court nominated by virtue of section 46(2)(a) to (c) of the Act; and
(b) an appeal from a decision of a district judge shall be heard by a circuit judge.

Amendments—Provision revoked with effect from 6 April 2015 by virtue of SI 2015/548 (subject to transitional provisions).

Appeals to the Court of Appeal

181 Appeals against decision of a puisne judge of the High Court, etc

(1) Where the decision sought to be appealed is a decision of a judge nominated by virtue of section 46(2)(a) to (c) of the Act, an appeal will lie only to the Court of Appeal.

(2) The judge nominated by virtue of section 46(2)(a) to (c) of the Act may grant permission to appeal to the Court of Appeal in accordance with this Part, where the decision sought to be appealed was a decision made by a judge so nominated as a first instance judge.

Amendments—Provision revoked with effect from 6 April 2015 by virtue of SI 2015/548 (subject to transitional provisions).

182 Second appeals

(1) A decision of a judge of the court which was itself made on appeal from a judge of the court may only be appealed further to the Court of Appeal.

(2) Permission is required from the Court of Appeal for such an appeal.

(3) The Court of Appeal will not give permission unless it considers that –

- *(a) the appeal would raise an important point of principle or practice; or*
- *(b) there is some other compelling reason for the Court of Appeal to hear it.*

(4) Nothing in this rule or in rule 181 applies to a second appeal from a decision of a nominated officer.

Amendments—Provision revoked with effect from 6 April 2015 by virtue of SI 2015/548 (subject to transitional provisions).

PART 21
ENFORCEMENT

183 Enforcement methods – general

(1) The rules in this Part make provision for the enforcement of judgments and orders.

(2) The relevant practice direction may set out methods of enforcing judgments or orders.

(3) An application for an order for enforcement may be made on application by any person in accordance with Part 10.

184 Application of the Civil Procedure Rules 1998 *and RSC Orders*

The following provisions apply, as far as they are relevant and with such modifications as may be necessary, to the enforcement of orders made in proceedings under these Rules –

- (a) Parts 70 (General Rules about Enforcement of Judgments and Orders), 71 (Orders to Obtain Information from Judgment Debtors), 72 (Third Party Debt Orders) *and*[,] 73 (Charging Orders, Stop Orders and Stop Notices)[,

83 (Writs and Warrants – General Provisions) and 84 (Enforcement by Taking Control of Goods)] of the Civil Procedure Rules 1998*; and*[.]

(b) *Orders 45 (Enforcement of Judgments and Orders: General), 46 (Writs of Execution: General) and 47 (Writs of Fieri Facias) of the Rules of the Supreme Court.*

Amendments—Words in italics revoked and words in square brackets inserted with effect from 1 July 2015 by virtue of SI 2015/548.

Orders for committal

185 Contempt of court – generally

An application relating to the committal of a person for contempt of court shall be made to a judge and the power to punish for contempt may be exercised by an order of committal.

186 Application for order of committal

(1) An application for an order of committal must be made by filing an application notice, stating the grounds of the application, and must be supported by an affidavit made in accordance with the relevant practice direction.

(2) Subject to paragraph (3), the application notice, a copy of the affidavit in support thereof and notice of the date of the hearing of the application must be served personally on the person sought to be committed.

(3) Without prejudice to its powers under Part 6, the court may dispense with service under this rule if it thinks it just to do so.

187 Oral evidence

If on the hearing of the application the person sought to be committed expresses a wish to give oral evidence on his own behalf, he shall be entitled to do so.

188 Hearing for committal order

(1) Except where the court permits, no grounds shall be relied upon at the hearing except the grounds set out in the application notice.

(2) Notwithstanding rule 90(1) (general rule – hearing to be in private), when determining an application for committal the court will hold the hearing in public unless it directs otherwise.

(3) If the court hearing an application in private decides that a person has committed a contempt of court, it shall state publicly –

(a) the name of that person;
(b) in general terms the nature of the contempt in respect of which the order of committal is being made; and
(c) any punishment imposed.

(4) If the person sought to be committed does not attend the hearing, the court may fix a date and time for the person to be brought before the court.

189 Power to suspend execution of committal order

(1) A judge who has made an order of committal may direct that the execution of the order of committal shall be suspended for such period or on such terms and conditions as may be specified.

(2) Where an order is suspended under paragraph (1), the applicant for the order of committal must, unless the court otherwise directs, serve on the person against whom it was made a notice informing him of the making and terms of the direction under that paragraph.

190 Warrant for arrest

A warrant for the arrest of a person against whom an order of committal has been made shall not, without further order of the court, be enforced more than 2 years after the date on which the warrant is issued.

191 Discharge of person committed

(1) The court may, on the application of any person committed to prison for contempt of court, discharge him.

(2) Where a person has been committed for failing to comply with a judgment or order requiring him to deliver any thing to some other person or to deposit it in court or elsewhere, and a writ of sequestration has also been issued to enforce that judgment or order, then, if the thing is in the custody or power of the person committed, the commissioners appointed by the writ of sequestration may take possession of it as if it were the property of that person and, without prejudice to the generality of paragraph (1), the court may discharge the person committed and may give such directions for dealing with the thing taken by the commissioners as it thinks fit.

192 Penal notices

(1) The court may direct that a penal notice is to be attached to any order warning the person on whom the copy of the order is served that disobeying the order would be a contempt of court punishable by imprisonment or a fine.

(2) Unless the court gives a direction under paragraph (1), a penal notice may not be attached to any order.

(3) A penal notice is to be in the following terms: 'You must obey this order. If you do not, you may be sent to prison for contempt of court.'.

193 Saving for other powers

The rules in this Part do not limit the power of the court to make an order requiring a person guilty of contempt to pay a fine or give security for his good behaviour and those rules, so far as applicable, shall apply in relation to an application for such an order as they apply in relation to an application for an order of committal.

194 Power of court to commit on its own initiative

The preceding provisions of these Rules shall not be taken as affecting the power of the court to make an order for committal on its own initiative against a person guilty of contempt of court.

PART 22
TRANSITORY AND TRANSITIONAL PROVISIONS

195 Transitory provision: applications by former receivers

(1) This rule and rule 196 –

(a) apply in any case where a person becomes a deputy by virtue of paragraph 1(2) of Schedule 5 to the Act; but
(b) shall cease to have effect at the end of the period specified in the relevant practice direction.

(2) The deputy may make an application to the court in connection with –

(a) any decision in connection with the day-to-day management of P's property and affairs; or
(b) any supplementary decision which is necessary to give full effect to any order made, or directions given, before 1 October 2007 under Part 7 of the Mental Health Act 1983.

(3) Decisions within paragraph (2) include those that may be specified in the relevant practice direction.

(4) An application –

(a) may relate only to a particular decision or decisions to be made on P's behalf;
(b) must specify details of the decision or decisions to be made; and
(c) must be made using the application form set out in the relevant practice direction.

196 Transitory provision: dealing with applications under rule 195

(1) The court may, in determining an application under rule 195, treat the application as if it were an application to vary the functions of the deputy which is made in accordance with the relevant practice direction made under rule 71, and dispose of it accordingly.

(2) In any other case, an application under rule 195 may be determined by an order made or directions given by –

(a) the court; or
(b) a person nominated under paragraph (3).

(3) The Senior Judge or the President may nominate an officer or officers of the court for the purpose of determining applications under rule 195.

(4) Where an officer has been nominated under paragraph (3) to determine an application, he may refer to a judge any proceedings or any question arising in any proceedings which ought, in the officer's opinion, to be considered by a judge.

197 Appeal against a decision of a nominated officer

(1) This rule applies in relation to decisions made under rules 195 and 196 by a nominated officer.

(2) An appeal from a decision to which this rule applies lies to a judge of the court nominated by virtue of section 46(2)(e) of the Act.

(3) No permission is required for an appeal under paragraph (2).

(4) A judge determining an appeal under paragraph (2) has all the powers that an appeal judge on appeal has by virtue of rule 178.

(5) An appeal from a decision made under paragraph (2) ('a second appeal') lies to a judge of the court nominated by virtue of section 46(2)(d) of the Act.

(6) A second appeal may be made from a decision of a nominated officer, and a judge to whom such an appeal is made may, if he considers the matter is one which ought to be heard by a judge of the court nominated by virtue of section 46(2)(a) to (c), transfer the matter to such a judge.

(7) An appeal from a decision made on a second appeal lies to the Court of Appeal.

198 Application of Rules to proceedings within paragraphs 3 and 12 of Schedule 5 to the Act

(1) In this rule, 'pending proceedings' means proceedings on an application within paragraph 3 or 12 of Schedule 5 to the Act.

(2) A practice direction shall make provision for the extent to which these Rules shall apply to pending proceedings.

199 Practice direction

A practice direction may make additional or different provision in relation to transitory and transitional matters.

PART 23
MISCELLANEOUS

200 Order or directions requiring a person to give security for discharge of functions

(1) This rule applies where the court makes an order or gives a direction –

- (a) conferring functions on any person (whether as deputy or otherwise); and
- (b) requiring him to give security for the discharge of those functions.

(2) The person on whom functions are conferred must give the security before he undertakes to discharge his functions, unless the court permits it to be given subsequently.

(3) Paragraphs (4) to (6) apply where the security is required to be given before any action can be taken.

(4) Subject to paragraph (5), the security must be given in accordance with the requirements of regulation 33(2)(a) of the Public Guardian Regulations (which

makes provision about the giving of security by means of a bond that is endorsed by an authorised insurance company or deposit-taker).

(5) The court may impose such other requirements in relation to the giving of the security as it considers appropriate (whether in addition to, or instead of, those specified in paragraph (4)).

(6) In specifying the date from which the order or directions referred to in paragraph (1) are to take effect, the court will have regard to the need to postpone that date for such reasonable period as would enable the Public Guardian to be satisfied that –

- (a) if paragraph (4) applies, the requirements of regulation 34 of the Public Guardian Regulations have been met in relation to the security; and
- (b) any other requirements imposed by the court under paragraph (5) have been met.

(7) 'The Public Guardian Regulations' means the Lasting Powers of Attorney, Enduring Powers of Attorney and Public Guardian Regulations 2007.

201 Objections to registration of an enduring power of attorney: request for directions

(1) This rule applies in any case where –

- (a) the Public Guardian (having received a notice of objection to the registration of an instrument creating an enduring power of attorney) is prevented by paragraph 13(5) of Schedule 4 to the Act from registering the instrument except in accordance with the court's directions; and
- (b) on or before the relevant day, no application for the court to give such directions has been made under Part 9 (how to start proceedings).

(2) In paragraph (1)(b) the relevant day is the later of –

- (a) the final day of the period specified in paragraph 13(4) of Schedule 4 to the Act; or
- (b) the final day of the period of 14 days beginning with the date on which the Public Guardian receives the notice of objection.

(3) The Public Guardian may seek the court's directions about registering the instrument by filing a request in accordance with the relevant practice direction.

(4) As soon as practicable and in any event within 21 days of the date on which the request was made, the court will notify –

- (a) the person (or persons) who gave the notice of objection; and
- (b) the attorney or, if more than one, each of them.

(5) As soon as practicable and in any event within 21 days of the date on which the request is filed, the Public Guardian must notify the donor of the power that the request has been so filed.

(6) The notice under paragraph (4) must –

- (a) state that the Public Guardian has requested the court's directions about registration;
- (b) state that the court will give directions in response to the request unless an application under Part 9 is made to it before the end of the period of 21 days commencing with the date on which the notice is issued; and
- (c) set out the steps required to make such an application.

(7) 'Notice of objection' means a notice of objection which is made in accordance with paragraph 13(4) of Schedule 4 to the Act.

202 Disposal of property where P ceases to lack capacity

(1) This rule applies where P ceases to lack capacity.

(2) In this rule, 'relevant property' means any property belonging to P and forming part of his estate, and which –

(a) remains under the control of anyone appointed by order of the court; or
(b) is held under the direction of the court.

(3) The court may at any time make an order for any relevant property to be transferred to P, or at P's direction, provided that it is satisfied that P has the capacity to make decisions in relation to that property.

(4) An application for an order under this rule is to be made in accordance with Part 10.